AN
CLOSENESS . . .

Abby rested her head on his shoulder and closed her eyes. She had thought that Kyle would be the first man to sweep her into his arms, carrying her, his bride, over the threshold into their new home. Not James Bradshaw, her academic rival, a man she barely knew and didn't even consider a friend.

And certainly not under these circumstances.

"We're almost there," he said.

Abby opened her eyes and studied Bradshaw's face, so close to hers she could've kissed his smooth, lean cheek if she wished. Which, she reminded herself hastily, she didn't. . . .

HEALING GIFTS

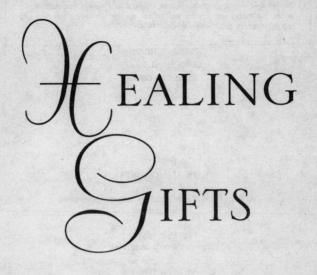

LESLIE BRANNEN

JOVE BOOKS, NEW YORK

HEALING GIFTS

A Jove Book / published by arrangement with
the author

PRINTING HISTORY
Jove edition / June 1998

All rights reserved.
Copyright © 1998 by Leslie Brannen.
This book may not be reproduced in whole
or in part, by mimeograph or any other means,
without permission. For information address:
The Berkley Publishing Group, a member of Penguin Putnam Inc.,
200 Madison Avenue, New York, New York 10016.

The Penguin Putnam Inc. World Wide Web site address is
http://www.penguinputnam.com

ISBN: 0-515-12288-2

A JOVE BOOK®
Jove Books are published by The Berkley Publishing Group,
a member of Penguin Putnam Inc.,
200 Madison Avenue, New York, New York 10016.
JOVE and the "J" design are trademarks belonging to
Jove Publications, Inc.

PRINTED IN THE UNITED STATES OF AMERICA

10 9 8 7 6 5 4 3 2 1

HEALING

GIFTS

1

CHICAGO, 1909

THE LAST PERSON ABBY EXPECTED TO FIND INVADing her refuge was James Bradshaw.

She had just returned to the boardinghouse from her final Monday afternoon class at the Chicago Veterinary College. She burst into the warm, welcoming foyer that still smelled sugary from the morning's baking, and shivered, her face stiff and cold. Abby wrestled the blustery November wind for the front door and won, closing it securely. Street sounds faded. Peace and quiet embraced her. She shed her heavy wool coat and headed for the kitchen to satisfy her craving for a pot of hot, soothing tea.

A man's laugh, deep and rich and unexpected, stopped her in her tracks.

Curious, she walked quietly down the narrow hallway to the parlor's arched entrance. She stepped inside, but her greeting died unspoken the second she recognized the well-dressed, black-haired man drinking tea so cozily with her landlady on the Stickley sofa.

James Bradshaw, one of her adversaries.

Her landlady started when she noticed Abby standing in the doorway. A stout, round-faced woman in her late forties, Josephine Wachowski regarded her with maternal concern.

"My goodness, Abigail," Josie said, setting down her favorite Chicago Exposition souvenir teacup, "I've never seen your cheeks so red. You must be freezing. Come join us for a nice hot cup of tea before you catch your death." She glanced at the man sitting next to her. "I believe you already know Mr. Bradshaw."

Bradshaw rose, his piercing onyx-eyed stare wide with surprise and puzzlement. "Miss Cooper. What are you doing here?"

"I might ask you the same question." She entered the parlor and walked over to the sofa. "Mrs. Wachowski didn't tell you that I live here?"

Josie patted the graying blond hair that she always wore in an old-fashioned coronet. "I may have neglected to mention it."

"Not that it matters," Bradshaw said.

Resentment raised Abby's hackles. How dare he make himself so comfortable in *her* home, dominating the small parlor with his tall, commanding presence, his supreme ease. He reminded Abby of a bold wolf staking out his territory.

She raised her brows. "I'm assuming you're not here on a social call."

He smiled. "Hardly."

"I've just rented Mr. Bradshaw the other room," Josie said.

Abby felt as though the floor had just opened up and

swallowed her. She looked over at Josie. "You didn't."

"I most certainly did." Josie noticed her guest's tea-cup was half-empty and poured him another cup. "Mr. Bradshaw's landlord needs his room for his ailing mother, and wants him out by tonight, poor man."

Bradshaw looked down at Josie and smiled. "Luckily for me, you had a room available."

Abby folded her arms to keep them from shaking. She didn't trust him. He'd do something to sabotage her studies. For all she knew, the other men in the class put him up to this, to spy on her.

She had to talk Josie out of renting him the room. Abby's peace of mind depended on it.

"Josie, may I speak to you a moment?" She glanced at Bradshaw. "In private."

"Of course." Josie rose in a rustle of long skirts. "If you'll excuse us, Mr. Bradshaw . . ."

Josie followed her out of the parlor and down the hall. When Abby was sure their conversation couldn't be overheard, she stopped and confronted her landlady.

She forced herself to keep her voice low. "Whatever possessed you to rent that room to the likes of James Bradshaw?"

"His landlord is evicting him. The poor man has no-where else to go."

Poor man indeed. "Surely this can't be the only boardinghouse near the college."

Josie's face softened, and she placed a soothing hand on Abby's arm. "There, there. I know the men in your class haven't made it easy for you, and many of them have been petty and cruel, but don't you think you're being unduly mistrustful of Mr. Bradshaw?"

Abby bristled. "I don't trust any of them. Why should I?"

"Has he ever picked on you, like the others? I don't recall your mentioning him."

"No," Abby admitted, "but he hasn't leaped to my defense, either." Her stomach knotted. "If he knew who stole my anatomy-class term paper last semester, he didn't say. At least the professor gave me some extra time to rewrite it, otherwise I would've failed the class. Who else but one of the men would've stolen it?

"And what about those two thugs who abducted me so I'd miss my final veterinary clinic exam?"

The nightmare was still as vivid as if it had happened yesterday. When she closed her eyes, she relived the day those two rough, remorseless men had abducted her right off the street in broad daylight, pulling and pushing her into a closed carriage, tying her hands so she couldn't fight, gagging her so she couldn't scream. She remembered the musty smell of the dark, abandoned building, sour and stale with disuse, where they kept her until nightfall, then released her, along with dire warnings not to talk.

But she had. To the police. To the college officials, who dismissed the incident as nothing more than a schoolboy prank carried too far.

Her abductors had frightened her badly, but not enough to make her quit. She had returned to class the next day with her nerves shot, but her head held high and backbone stiff with determination. The college officials allowed her to take the missed exam. She scored higher than any man in her class, including James Bradshaw.

The police had never caught the instigator. Those who knew his identity upheld their conspiracy of silence.

But in a way, they won. Sometimes, in the middle of the night, Abby would awake from a deep sleep screaming in mind-numbing terror, bathed in icy sweat, her racing, pounding heart ready to explode out of her chest.

Josie sighed regretfully. "That was terrible, just terrible, but I can't bring myself to believe that Mr. Bradshaw had anything to do with what happened to you." Josie simply couldn't believe the worst of any man so charming and good looking.

Abby folded her arms. "Perhaps he didn't, but I can't afford to take any chances." She leaned forward. "Please, Josie. Don't rent the room to him. For my sake."

Josie sighed again. "I'm sorry, Abigail, but I already have. We have an arrangement, and he's already paid me for the first month. You know I never go back on my word." When Abby exhaled a sharp sigh of frustration, Josie said, "It won't be so bad. You'll still have your own room. You'll come and go as you please. You'll never have to see each other, except for meals. Please try to see this situation from my point of view."

Josie just didn't understand. The boardinghouse had been Abby's refuge, her oasis of solitude and peace. Now she would be sharing it with one of the very men who wanted the college's first female veterinary student to fail.

"But what do you really know about him?" she pointed out. "I've been going to school with him for three years, and all I know is that he's insufferable and arrogant."

"Mr. Bradshaw has provided me with several excellent references," Josie said, "all attesting to the fact that he's quiet and studious. I told him I hold my tenants to the highest standards, and will not tolerate drunkenness or entertaining loose women in my house.

"Besides, this house should have a man. We're two

women living alone, and I fear for our safety, especially after what happened to you. Any kidnappers or burglars will think twice if they see a tall, strong man coming and going.''

Abby could see this was one battle she wouldn't win.

"It is your house," she said stiffly. "You may rent to whomever you please. But James Bradshaw had better stay out of my way.''

Without another word, she headed for the kitchen to make herself that soothing pot of tea.

Once upstairs in the solitude of her own room, Abby set the tea tray down on her desk and sat on the edge of her bed so she could look at the photographs arranged on the nightstand: one of her parents together, another of her mother and her horse, and a third of Kyle Lambert, the man Abby loved and planned to marry.

A wave of homesickness swept over her as she picked up Kyle's photograph. Taken with him standing proudly behind the bar at One-Eyed Jack's, the saloon he ran back in Little Falls, Missouri, even his serious, unsmiling expression couldn't hide the laughter and mischief in his eyes.

Even though Abby's parents and grandmother had reservations about Kyle just because he ran a saloon, she loved him and missed him terribly. She couldn't wait to graduate, open her own veterinary practice back in Little Falls, and marry Kyle.

She placed his photo back, rose, and stared down at her mother's picture. Taken by the renowned photographer Dennis Dunleavy when Catherine Wills Cooper was only twenty-one, a year younger than Abby was now, the photograph showed her standing beside her beloved black mare.

"You warned me that vet school would be tough, Mama," she whispered. "You told me the men would resent me, and make my life hell. And they have. But I've gotten this far, and not only am I going to graduate, I'm going to be valedictorian. I'm going to beat them all, Mr. James Bradshaw included."

A loud knock made her jump. "Yes?"

"Miss Cooper," came Bradshaw's deep, muffled voice, "I want to have a word with you about your cat."

Abby flung open her door to find Bradshaw grimacing in pain and pressing a handkerchief against the back of his hand. "Ulysses? What have you done to my cat?"

"Nothing. He came into my room, and scratched me when I tried to pet him," he said.

"You of all people should know better than to try to touch a strange animal," she retorted, sailing past him with her chin in the air and marching across the hall.

Bradshaw followed. "That animal's vicious."

Kyle thought him vicious as well, but then, he preferred dogs to cats.

"He is not vicious. He just doesn't like you."

"A quality he obviously shares with his mistress."

Abby ignored that comment as she searched the spacious room, unmindful of the fact that she was a single woman alone in a gentleman's bedroom.

She spied Ulysses sitting on his haunches atop the bureau, his long skinny tail curled around him as he blithely washed his front paw.

"There's the little devil," Bradshaw muttered. "Licking my blood off his claws."

"Stop being such a baby," Abby said. "That scratch won't kill you."

"Sorry to disappoint you."

Ulysses stopped washing and watched the exchange

out of curious green eyes. Abby thought him a handsome, distinguished-looking three-year-old feline, with thick white fur splashed with black on his chest and haunches, and a comical soot-colored smudge covering his nose and mouth.

"Well, we don't get everything we want in life, do we?" she snapped.

Abby extended her hands. "Poor Ulysses," she crooned, lifting him gently off the bureau and cradling his soft, furry body in her arms. "Did the strange man scare you?" Ulysses mewed plaintively in agreement.

Bradshaw raised his brows. "Ulysses?"

"He was named after Ulysses S. Grant," Abby informed him with a disdainful sniff.

She had no intention of telling him that her family always kept a cat named Ulysses in memory of its ancestor who bedeviled Abby's grandmother's coonhound years ago.

"Ulysses has the run of the house," she continued. "He also likes to come in this room because there's a mousehole in the wall near the foot of your bed." Abby kissed the top of her cat's head. "Ulysses is the best mouser in Chicago."

"Just make sure you keep the General out of my room. I don't want to be scratched again."

She hugged Ulysses protectively, pressing his face against her cheek. He purred. She glared at Bradshaw. "If you keep your door closed, he'll stay out."

"I intend to."

"Don't complain if you should hear mice scurrying across your floor at night."

"I won't. If your cat should sneak in again, you're going to have to remove him."

"If you don't want to be scratched again, give him a wide berth."

Bradshaw removed his handkerchief and stared down at the two long, deep scratches running down the back of his hand from the base of his fingers to his wrist. "Don't worry. I won't give him a second chance to maul me."

Abby headed for the open door. Just when she reached it, Bradshaw called her name. She stopped and turned. "Yes?"

He grinned. "Has anyone ever told you that your eyes turn green when you're angry?"

Damn him. She thought of Kyle and smiled slowly, smugly. "As a matter of fact, someone has."

She turned without waiting to see his reaction, and walked out of the room.

James finished unpacking his bags and smiled in satisfaction. Mrs. Wachowski's boardinghouse suited him perfectly. The homey ordinariness and warmth drew him like a magnet, from the cheap, machine-made mission furniture cluttering every room to all the souvenirs from the Chicago Exposition Mrs. Wachowski displayed as proudly as if they were priceless objets d'art. His own room was spacious, the street below was relatively quiet, and the rent reasonable. Perfect—well almost.

Perfect except for Miss Abigail "Ice Maiden" Cooper.

James had never met a colder, more remote female. Or one more intelligent.

In every class, she arrived first and left last, always sitting warily in the last row, in the seat nearest the door, with her back to the wall. She studiously took notes and never spoke to her classmates. Some regarded her with ill-concealed hostility, and others indifference. Yet whenever the professor called on her, she knew the answers, and they were always exasperatingly, infuriatingly correct.

He smiled as he started down the stairs to go to dinner. He preferred women who were softer and warmer, but he had to admit that he enjoyed the exhilaration of their verbal sparring. She argued logically and directly, without heat and without mercy, her sharp mind working like a well-oiled machine.

But like a well-oiled machine, she lacked a heart.

Except when it came to animals. He had to admit Miss Cooper had a talent for soothing the most savage beast.

As he approached the kitchen, he heard a woman's light, carefree laugh. He paused in the hallway just out of sight of Abigail Cooper standing at the black, cast-iron stove, ladling steaming soup into bowls and handing them to Mrs. Wachowski. The remnants of a rare smile lingered on her full, rosy mouth and a gleam of humor warmed those cool blue eyes.

James studied her, intrigued to have caught the Ice Maiden at an unguarded moment. She was every inch the modern, emancipated female, the New Woman, and a dead ringer for the Gibson girl. Unlike Mrs. Wachowski, who clung to her dated shirtwaist with its puffy leg-o'-mutton sleeves and a long, full skirt, the brash Miss Cooper dressed with defiance. No boned high collar immobilized her head like a vise. Her collarless blouse revealed an enticing expanse of long, white neck, and her five-gore skirt accented her narrow waist and slim hips.

The minute she glanced over and caught him staring, her smile died. An angry blush suffused that graceful neck and crept up her cheeks. He could almost see ice crystals forming.

"Dinner will be served in the dining room, Mr. Bradshaw," Mrs. Wachowski said with a smile.

Once they were all seated at the dining room table and commenced eating, James complimented his landlady profusely on the delicious chicken soup that warmed him all the way down to his toes. Then he looked at Miss Cooper, seated across from him. "Are you from the Chicago area?"

"No."

He waited. She sipped her soup. He waited. She took another sip. Stubborn.

He raised a mocking brow. "Cat got your tongue, Miss Cooper?"

Her blue eyes turned an angry shade of green. She said nothing.

Mrs. Wachowski flashed an alarmed look at her rude tenant. "Both of us are from Little Falls, Missouri, though I came to Chicago to live with relatives when I was just a little girl, after my parents were killed."

"Killed?" In an accident, he assumed. An overturned carriage, a flood, a fire. Mundane hazards of country living.

"They were shot by bushwackers," Mrs. Wachowski said matter-of-factly, without the sorrow of a recent loss. "I was only seven at the time. My sisters and I ran off into the woods near our farm and escaped."

Murder. Something that had touched James's own life once too often in his twenty-five years.

"How horrible," he said softly. He remembered Mrs. Wachowski telling him earlier that she had four younger sisters, all scattered around the country except for one, who lived in Evanston.

"Abby's grandparents found us," she said. "We were scared half out of our wits, and Maddy and Dr. Paul were so kind. Later, these same bushwackers shot Maddy when they held up the bank. She was luckier than my folks. She survived."

At the mention of her grandmother, Abby Cooper's guarded expression softened for a fleeting instant. A spark in all that ice, an unexpected gentleness.

James shook his head. "I always thought small towns were peaceful and quiet."

"They are." The Ice Maiden finally spoke, surprising him. "The last crime committed in Little Falls happened this summer, when Helmut Blick threw a stone at the mercantile's new window and broke it."

To consider breaking a window a horrendous crime . . . James almost burst out laughing. So beneath that suit of armor breathed an innocent farm girl. Interesting.

Miss Cooper finished her soup. "These days, there's more violence in Chicago than in Little Falls."

He knew that all too well.

"Little Falls sounds like paradise." He met her startled gaze squarely. He could tell she hadn't expected him to say that. "Why did you leave small-town life for the anonymity and bustle of the big city?"

Impatience flared in her eyes. "To attend veterinary school, of course."

"Of course." Now that he'd gotten her to relax her guard and open up a bit, he pressed. "Why did you want to become a vet?"

"I imagine for the same reason you did."

No, he couldn't imagine they shared the same dark, driving force to succeed.

Mrs. Wachowski asked him if he wanted more soup, and when he regretfully declined, she said, "Veterinarians run in Abby's family. Not only was her grandfather—God rest his soul—one, but her grandmother and her mother, too.''

James dabbed at his lips with his napkin. ''How can that be? Women haven't been admitted to vet schools until recently.''

''As my mother found out, when she tried to enroll some years ago,'' Miss Cooper said, glaring at him as if he were personally responsible. ''My grandmother healed animals with herbs and my mother learned veterinary medicine from her parents. I'll be the first vet in the family to receive a degree.''

She looked as though she intended to say more, caught herself before she revealed too much, and fell silent.

''Abigail is going to be valedictorian,'' Mrs. Wachowski said proudly.

James smiled. ''Not if I can help it.''

At the landlady's confused look, Miss Cooper said, ''Mr. Bradshaw has the second-highest grade-point average in our class.''

''There's still plenty of time for me to surpass you and become valedictorian,'' he said, enjoying the faint flush of anger tinting her cheeks.

''Wishful thinking, Mr. Bradshaw?'' She rose and collected the empty soup bowls. ''You sit right there, Josie. I'll get the stuffed cabbage.''

They were the best James had ever eaten. Mrs. Wachowski's cooking was yet another reason to stay, whether or not the coldhearted Miss Cooper approved.

Truth be told, she intrigued him.

Yes, he thought, helping himself to another slice of rye bread, life in Mrs. Wachowski's boardinghouse was going to prove interesting.

• • •

James closed his textbook, pushed the chair away from the desk, and yawned. He glanced at the clock. Nearly midnight. If he wanted to be fresh and sharp for class tomorrow, he had better get to bed.

He rose and stretched, causing the scratches on his hand to sting. He winced. Damn that cat. A picture of Abigail Cooper, her soft cloud of dark hair framing her pale, indignant face, looking like a witch protecting her familiar, danced through his mind and made him smile.

Suddenly he realized that he'd been so absorbed in his studies that he'd failed to pull down the shades. He walked over to the big bay window. Just as he was about to draw the shades, a familiar, stoop-shouldered figure in the street below caught his eye.

The man's hands were jammed into the deep pockets of a dark overcoat so big and shapeless that it could hide a small arsenal. He strolled in front of the Wachowski house much too slowly for a bitterly cold Chicago night, then stopped at the foot of the steep steps. He studied the house with the keen-eyed absorption of a burglar searching for a carelessly unlocked window or door.

The streetlight clearly illuminated his familiar, lugubrious face.

Parson Brown.

James dashed out of his room, barely noticing the thread of yellow light beneath Miss Cooper's door. He groped the wall as carefully as a blind man down the unlit stairs, praying he didn't trip and fall headlong into the dark, yawning chasm. Once downstairs, he ran across the foyer, unlocked the front door, and flung it open.

The Parson had vanished.

James swore under his breath and ran down the front

steps, recoiling as a wall of frigid air slammed into him, causing him to gasp in shock. He looked up and down the street at empty doorways and dark, gaping alleys, but the man was gone.

Teeth chattering from cold and frustration, James turned. He glanced back at the house. There stood Abigail Cooper silhouetted in her window, watching him. She turned away.

Seconds later, her light went out.

2

THE FOLLOWING MORNING, ABBY AWOKE TO THE relentless kneading of Ulysses' front paws on her shoulder. He stopped when he saw he'd accomplished his daily duty of waking her, closed his eyes, and rubbed his face against her cheek.

She didn't need to look at the clock on her nightstand to know the time, for Ulysses always performed this particular ritual faithfully at seven o'clock, seven days a week including Saturday and Sunday, no matter what the season.

"I know, I know," Abby grumbled, stifling a yawn. "You want your breakfast."

In the three years since Abby had been living in Chicago, she had gotten used to the city's incessant sounds of delivery wagons rumbling at all hours outside her window, and could now sleep through them. Even the shriek of the six o'clock whistle from the shoe factory several blocks away seldom woke her. But she couldn't ignore her persistent cat.

She scratched Ulysses behind the ears. He closed his round green eyes into slanted slits of feline euphoria, and purred loudly. The minute Abby began moving her foot beneath the covers, the cat's eyes sprang open in curiosity at the menacing rustle. He crouched as still as a fierce jungle tiger, his ears pricked forward and every sense honed to razor sharpness, as the threatening mound inched closer. Closer.

"What's that?" Abby whispered excitedly, enjoying their morning game as much as he. "A big, tasty mouse from Mr. Bradshaw's bedroom? Yum!"

At her goading, Ulysses flicked the tip of his tail once, just before he sprang, but Abby's reflexes were quicker and she moved her foot away just in time. The cat bounded and shot after the retreating lump, eager for the kill. He pounced, grasping Abby's foot with tooth and claw.

"Okay, that's enough," she said, grateful for the thick covers' protection as she stilled and flattened her foot, then pushed him away. "Game's over."

Ulysses darted left, then pirouetted gracefully on his hind legs, searching every inch of the bed for his prey, but the big mouse had vanished, eluding him yet again. The cat stilled, looked at Abby, and meowed plaintively.

She kept her expression deadpan. "I don't know where it went."

"Yes, you do," Ulysses' frustrated expression seemed to say as he stepped gingerly across the covers and returned to Abby's side.

She sat up and drew him into her lap, savoring his warmth and soft, thick fur beneath her calming, stroking hand. "Maybe you'll have better luck tomorrow morning."

Ulysses glared disdainfully, then took a chastising swipe at the blue satin ribbon tying her long braid, just to let her know exactly what he thought of her false promise.

Abby scratched him beneath the chin, then set him aside so she could get ready for school.

When she threw back the covers, she shivered from the chill in the room. She slid her bare feet into slippers before they could turn to ice on the cold wood floor, then put on the warm flannel kimono her sister Lizzie had given her last Christmas.

Abby went to the window to see if any snow had fallen overnight. Much to her relief, the street was still dry. Yesterday's flat gray sky had broken up into scudding white clouds revealing patches of brilliant blue. A reprieve.

As she looked across the street at the meat wagon parked in the alley adjacent to Kachinsky's Butcher Shop to unload raw, skinned sides of beef, she recalled last night, when James Bradshaw had gone running out of the house.

Abby had been studying at her desk when she heard Bradshaw's door open, followed by loud, hurried footsteps disappearing down the hall. Curious, she opened her own door and listened. When she heard the front door slam, she went to her own window.

Bradshaw stood coatless at the foot of the stairs, and scanned the street like Ulysses on the prowl. Then he turned and looked up, the streetlight momentarily illuminating his hard, furious expression.

Abby had felt a shudder of fear for whoever had sent James Bradshaw racing out into the cold and wind at midnight.

Now, standing at her window with her arms folded, she wondered if she should confront him.

''What good would it do?'' she muttered to Ulysses,

pacing back and forth by the closed door and looking up at her expectantly. "He's not about to tell me the truth."

She would tell Josie, and let her decide what to do.

Abby glanced at the clock. She'd better wash and dress, or she'd be late for her first class. Infectious diseases, her favorite.

She opened her door and peered down the hall while her cat darted out. When she saw the coast was clear, she hurried into the bathroom at the far end and locked the door behind her, feeling as triumphant as Ulysses' namesake taking Richmond.

No sooner did she draw a hot bath laced with aromatic salts and step into the rose-scented water for a long, leisurely soak, than there came an imperious knock on the door.

"Don't dawdle, Miss Cooper," Bradshaw said. "You're not the only one living here, you know."

Abby gritted her teeth and resisted the impulse to fling her sopping washcloth at the door. "I'll be done in a minute."

Ten minutes later, she emerged from the steam-fogged bathroom wrapped in her kimono to find Bradshaw waiting impatiently. Partially unbuttoned, his bathrobe revealed a vee of hard male chest sleek with short, straight hairs.

Abby was not a woman usually ruffled by the sight of a half-dressed man, accustomed as she was to seeing shirtless men working on her family's horse farm. Men mending fences under a blazing August sun that burned and bronzed their muscular shoulders. Men shoeing horses, the withering blast from the forge glossing their faces and arms with sweat. She had even seen Kyle shirtless once, and experienced the first sweet stirrings of desire at his physical perfection.

But there was something about James Bradshaw wrapped in his bathrobe that imprisoned her gaze and made embarrassment blossom in her cheeks.

"About time," he muttered, his annoyed glance taking in her kimono.

Abby grasped one end of the towel draped around her neck and dabbed at her face to hide her embarrassment as she walked past. "It's a steam bath in there."

"Must be why your cheeks are so red," he said with a knowing grin.

Abby stopped and turned. She reached over to the light switch and turned on the hallway's overhead light. "There's a switch at either end of the hall, just in case you have to leave your room at midnight again."

Abby turned and marched back to her room. Damn the man's insufferable conceit, acting as though the mere sight of him in his bathrobe would leave her swooning at his feet. Well, at least she had made it clear that she knew all about his nocturnal foray.

When she reached her door, she glanced back down the hall. Bradshaw was standing in the bathroom doorway, watching her, his expression unreadable.

Abby entered her room and made her bed then dressed in a white lawn shirtwaist and dark brown five-gored skirt before putting up her hair. When she finished, she made sure she locked her bedroom door before going down to breakfast.

The empty, overheated classroom smelled faintly of ink, chalk dust, and hot radiators as it awaited the next wave of students.

Abby took off her coat and went to her customary

first seat in the last row. When she had started college, she foolishly sat at the head of the class, to better observe the professor. After having her hat knocked off "accidentally" several times, and ink "accidentally" spilled all over her notes, not to mention the spitballs that "accidentally" flew through the air and landed in her hair, Abby prudently retreated.

This didn't stop the more hostile male students from tormenting her. Once she found a harmless garter snake coiled on her chair, and a room full of men waiting for her to scream or faint. She disappointed them by picking up the reptile and letting it slither from hand to hand as she coldly informed the class that it was a measure of their ignorance to assume that all women feared snakes. Especially a woman who intended to become a veterinarian.

When the abduction didn't force her out, the pranks stopped. Abby sensed the perpetrator still lurking in the wings, marshaling his resources, just waiting for another chance.

No sooner did she open her notebook to review the last lecture than her male classmates entered the room, some alone, and others in laughing, joking groups. Most ignored Abby. Several smiled and nodded. She responded in kind.

Though absorbed in her notes, she became aware of someone sitting down next to her.

"Why didn't you wait for me?" Bradshaw said. "I would've walked over with you."

"Thank you for the offer, but it's not necessary," Abby replied, keeping her eyes on her notes. "I know the way."

Before Bradshaw could comment, Abby's chief tormentor, Rockwell Shays and his two toadies, breezed into the room as if they owned it.

Abby couldn't understand why a young man blessed with intelligence, charm, looks, and family wealth took perverse delight in harassing her. She'd never done anything to him.

She stiffened instinctively as Shays stopped by her seat, but she wouldn't look away. To her relief, he said, "Hey, Bradshaw, what are you doing back here with *her*? Aren't you afraid you'll catch fleas?"

He and his friends guffawed.

"That's enough, Shays." Bradshaw's tone would've frozen fire.

The men stopped laughing.

Shays's eyes narrowed. "Well, I'll be . . . you're going over to her side."

"I'm not on anyone's side," he replied.

Before Shays could continue, Dr. Phineas Hogg appeared in the doorway, signaling for everyone to take their seats.

Abby glanced at Bradshaw. Why had he come to her defense just now? He never had in the past three years. He must have had an ulterior motive.

Dr. Hogg, nicknamed "Piggy" by his students, set his books on his desk and sat on the edge. A short, thin man in his late fifties, with graying brown hair that stuck out every which way like a boar-bristle brush, Dr. Hogg adjusted his colorful bow tie, signaling that the class had better come to order.

"I have a sick dog," Professor Hogg began. He was fond of testing the class with hypothetical examples. "His symptoms include rapid tiring, excessive sweating, and difficulty breathing. Later, he stops eating, but becomes excessively thirsty."

Dr. Hogg offered a list of additional symptoms, saying, "A chronic swelling of the lymph glands appears symmetrically on both sides of the body. The spleen becomes enlarged." He looked around the room. "So, Miss Cooper and gentlemen, tell me what's wrong with my dog."

Shays raised his hand. When Hogg called on him, he rose and said, "I would make a diagnosis of leukemia, sir."

"Would you, now?" The professor's bland expression revealed nothing. "Would you tell the class how you arrived at your diagnosis, Mr. Shays?"

"Swollen lymph glands is one of the major symptoms of leukemia," he replied.

"True, but they're also a symptom of glanders, tuberculosis, and malignant tumors." He shifted his gaze to the left. "Miss Cooper, do you agree with Mr. Shays's diagnosis?"

Abby rose. "Before I answer, may I ask a question, sir?"

"You may."

"If I were to draw this dog's blood, what would be its characteristics?"

"On coagulating, it would separate into two layers. The lower layer would be violet-colored, and the upper layer grayish white and milklike."

Abby took a deep breath. "And upon examining the upper layer under a microscope, would I see an increase in the number of white corpuscles?"

Dr. Hogg shook his head. "No."

"Then my diagnosis would not be leukemia at all, but *pseudo*leukemia."

A smile tugged at Dr. Hogg's mouth and made his

bristle of a mustache twitch. "How did you reach such a diagnosis?"

"The symptoms of leukemia and pseudoleukemia are exactly the same," Abby said, "except for the fact that only leukemia shows an increase in the white blood cell count. Pseudoleukemia does not."

"Correct," the professor said, beaming.

Several of the men groaned, obviously not pleased to hear Abby give the right answer. Shays turned in his seat and glared at her, his cold, disapproving stare threatening retribution.

Shays raised his hand, and when the professor called on him again, he rose and said, "I object, Dr. Hogg. You didn't give us all the information we needed before you asked for a diagnosis."

The professor raised his bushy brows almost to the hairline. "Come, come, Mr. Shays, don't be a sore loser. You could've thought to ask me about the blood's white corpuscle count just as Miss Cooper did, but you didn't."

"I realize now that I should have, sir," he said, before sitting down.

"Yes, you should've." The professor gave his class a look of stern reproach. "When you become practicing veterinarians, Miss Cooper and gentlemen, I'm not going to be around to give you all the information you'll need to make a diagnosis. You're going to have to learn it all, and remember it."

Shays raised his hand again, and when the professor called on him, he rose. "Why do we have to know the difference? Whether the animal contracts leukemia or pseudoleukemia, it's still going to die."

Dr. Hogg grabbed fistfuls of his own hair and grimaced theatrically as he pretended to pull it out by the roots. His eyes blazed. "Because we are scientists, you dolt! We seek to acquire knowledge, not just make a diagnosis and collect our fee." He looked around the room. "Perhaps one of you will discover a cure for leukemia, but you'll never accomplish such a feat if you can't even recognize it."

A resentful Shays slunk down like a whipped dog into his seat, then turned to glare at Abby as if his being called a dolt was somehow her fault.

Though she kept her expression neutral and her gaze trained on Dr. Hogg, she sensed that Shays was planning some fresh torment for her, and she'd better be on her guard.

Dr. Hogg glanced at the wall clock. "That's all for today, class. I'll see you in lab tomorrow." He grinned wickedly, baring large, tobacco-stained teeth. "If you know what's good for you."

Abby rose, put on her coat, gathered her books, and was out the door before most of the men had even risen. She had learned early that it was best to get a head start on the likes of Rockwell Shays rather than pin a target on her back and wait for the arrows to strike.

She was halfway down the hall before she heard Bradshaw calling her name. She turned and paused. "Yes, Mr. Bradshaw?"

"Are you going to surgical procedures?" he asked, joining her.

"That's a fair assumption, since it's our next class," she replied dryly, resuming walking.

Bradshaw smiled. "Then I'll walk with you, if you don't mind."

She lifted one shoulder. "Whatever." And kept on going.

Classroom doors along the corridor suddenly swung open, and students poured out into the hallway.

Without warning, someone bumped into Abby, jostling her.

"Sorry," the young man said before melting into the throng of students hurrying on to their next class.

Evans. One of Shays's toadies.

Abby barely had time to draw another breath and clutch her books tighter when she was bumped again from behind, harder this time, hard enough to push her against Bradshaw, who reached out to steady her.

When she regained her balance, she stopped right in the middle of the corridor and glowered at the perpetrator.

Hendries, Shays's other friend.

Before Abby could open her mouth, Bradshaw's arm shot out and he grabbed Hendries's shoulder. "Apologize to the lady."

Around them, the other students gave them wide berth, several casting curious glances before hurrying down the hall.

Hendries, a good head shorter and thirty pounds lighter than Bradshaw, swallowed hard when he saw that he wasn't going anywhere. "I'm so very, *very* sorry, my dear Miss Cooper," he said. "I should've been watching where I was going."

"Yes, you should have," Abby snapped, giving Hendries a look that could have peeled paint.

Bradshaw released him, and Hendries scurried off.

Heart pounding more in anger than fear, Abby backed over to the wall when she saw Shays lingering in a classroom doorway, obviously waiting for his chance to send her sprawling. She hated letting him see her with her back literally to the wall, but she'd be damned if she'd allow him to hurt her. If he tried, she'd swing her heavy book satchel as hard as she could and drive it right into his crotch.

"You'll be a young woman alone in a big, wicked city," her mother had warned her just before Abby left for Chicago. "You've got to watch out for yourself, because no one else will."

If Kyle were here, he would fling Rockwell Shays against the wall for daring to have his cronies shove Abby. But Kyle wasn't here.

Bradshaw joined Abby in keeping a watchful eye on Shays, who stepped out of the doorway and sauntered down the hall. He smirked at Abby as he passed, then disappeared down the stairs.

Abby took several deep breaths to settle her shaking insides, then marched down the hall, taking little notice of Bradshaw as he fell in step beside her.

He didn't say anything until they were outside. "I'm sorry you had to be subjected to that."

Abby's resentment and frustration at her own helplessness caused her temper to flare. She could almost feel the anger turning her eyes from blue to green. "Oh, spare me your apologies, Mr. Bradshaw. You're no better than the rest. For the past three years, you've watched Shays and his ilk torment me, trying to force me out of school, but you've never once tried to stop them. Except for today."

James winced. The truth hurt. He was no better than Shays. A cad, and a coward. Over the last three years, he had seen Hendries dump ink on Miss Cooper's notes, and had looked away when Shays sent a spitball shooting into her hair. While their bullying angered him, not once did he try to stop them.

It's not that he feared physical confrontation. He

feared that once he started, he wouldn't be able to stop.

But what had his mother always taught him, that if a man stands by and watches an injustice being committed, he's just as much to blame as the perpetrator?

"I guess I deserved that," he said.

He glanced at Miss Cooper striding down the sidewalk, her back ramrod straight and her armor of ice solidly in place. He could tell the encounter with Shays and his cronies had shaken her more than she wanted to admit.

She caught him watching her, and gave him an exasperated look. "Mr. Bradshaw, what are you *doing* here? I didn't ask you to follow me around."

"No, but Mrs. Wachowski did."

"She *what*?"

"She said we all had to stick together, and she asked me to keep an eye on you."

They reached Haddison Hall, where their next class was scheduled. Bradshaw opened the door for her.

"Josie means well," she said, "but I wish she wouldn't meddle."

"She's only concerned about you. Ever since you were abducted, she fears you'll be sold into white slavery."

The Ice Maiden dismissed her landlady's fears by rolling her eyes skyward. "I am not naive, Mr. Bradshaw. I know Chicago is a virtual Gomorrah, but I sometimes think Josie's unhealthy interest in this city's criminal elements is irrational."

But James knew differently.

3

"It's painful and inhumane," Bradshaw insisted, holding open the boardinghouse's front door for Abby, "to castrate a horse without chloroforming it first."

She brushed past him, eager for the hallway's warm embrace, for the temperature had fallen during the day, turning the late afternoon raw and colder.

She set her book bag down on the floor by the coatrack. "And I suppose it's more humane to risk asphyxiation from the anesthesia, or breaking the horse's neck or spine from casting when it's thrown down?"

"If the vet is skilled," he retorted, peeling off his black kidskin gloves, "the horse is perfectly safe."

Ever since their last class for the day, Abby and Bradshaw had been arguing between the merits of casting, throwing the horse to the ground using hobbles and ropes to control the animal during castration, and using a twitch on its sensitive upper lip to keep it immobile and on its feet while the vet performed the procedure.

"True, the horse feels pain without anesthesia," she said, unbuttoning her coat, "but I think that short-term pain is preferable to killing the animal."

To her surprise, Bradshaw moved to help her out of her coat. As he stood behind her and reached around, she felt his warm breath on her neck and his fingers brush her shoulders, his closeness disconcerting.

Bradshaw hung up her coat and turned, his dark eyes gleaming. The man certainly loved a good argument. "As a veterinarian, aren't you concerned about sparing animals pain?"

"Of course," she retorted, "but you're forgetting the animal's owner." She drifted toward the kitchen and her hot cup of after-school tea. "Someone who's paid hundreds, even thousands of dollars, for a horse has an investment to protect. Whether it's a millionaire who's just bought a very expensive pleasure horse, or a cabby who depends on a hack for his livelihood, he's going to want the procedure performed without killing the animal."

"So you're saying that the owner's wishes are what matters, not providing a pain-free procedure for the animal."

Abby gave him an exasperated look as they entered the kitchen. "All I'm saying is that we have to do what's best for both the animal and its owner, who, after all, is paying our bill."

"That sounds very mercenary of you, Miss Cooper."

Abby filled the teakettle with water and brought it over to the stove. "I merely see the argument from an owner's perspective. My family has been breeding horses since the Civil War, and I know my father has always preferred a live horse to a dead one. And my mother has done her share of castrations."

Bradshaw gave a mock shudder. "I hope your father stayed out of her way when she was in a bad mood."

Abby smiled in spite of herself. "She only castrated horses, and when she did, she later came to prefer using the twitch because there was less recovery time."

Bradshaw opened the cupboards and removed cups and saucers without being asked. "Preferred? She doesn't practice any more?"

"No. The responsibilities of raising three daughters and helping my father with the farm kept her too busy for general veterinary work, so she only treated the family's animals."

"Is that why you wanted to go to vet school? To accomplish what your mother didn't?"

Abby mentally kicked herself for allowing the warmth and intimacy of the kitchen to lull her into letting down her guard and loosening her tongue. He may have defended her against Shays today, but she still didn't trust him.

She regarded him coolly. "Why all the personal questions, Mr. Bradshaw?"

"I'm curious." He leaned back against the counter and folded his arms. "What drives you? What keeps you enduring all the disapproval, the petty harassment? Strength, or some inner demon?"

She looked at him. "Haven't you ever wanted something so badly you'll endure anything to get it?"

He grinned. "Yes, I have. But we were discussing you."

The kettle whistled.

Abby took it off the stove. "No, *you* were discussing me, and that discussion is at an end. I am going to take my tea upstairs to my room and start studying."

The sound of hurried footsteps coming down the hall caused both of them to look up. Several seconds later, Josie breezed into the kitchen.

"There you are," she said. "I was upstairs cleaning, and I didn't hear you two come in."

Bradshaw smiled. "You didn't hear us debating the merits of casting versus the twitch?"

Josie gave them a blank stare. "Casting? Does that have something to do with fishing?"

"No, not fishing," Abby said, giving Bradshaw a pointed, warning look. "Just something we're studying, that's all."

Josie took two letters from her apron pocket and handed them to Abby. "Mail from home. One from your grandmother and one from"—she gave Abby a dreamy-eyed smile—"your beloved."

A letter from Kyle. Abby's heart stuttered and skipped a beat. She felt her cheeks turn pink as she slipped the letters into her skirt pocket.

Abby tried to return to making tea, but it was no use. She had to read her letters at once, or she'd die.

She excused herself and strode out of the kitchen, anticipation quickening her steps. Whatever Bradshaw said to Josie to make her giggle girlishly, Abby didn't care to know. Her letters were all that mattered.

Upstairs in her bedroom, Abby sat down on the window seat and tore open Grandmama Maddy's letter first, for she wanted to read Kyle's letter later, saving the best for last. Still, she hungered for news from home, and her grandmother's letters were always a banquet of observations both sweet and tart.

The letter began with a few sentences about every member of the Cooper family. Abby's mother Catherine, nicknamed Cat, had twisted her ankle, but was on the mend. Abby's father, Michael, had sold another horse. Her insufferable younger sister, Regina, who was married to a banker and put on airs, had finally realized that even she would not be spared morning sickness with her second pregnancy. Lizzie, Abby's youngest sister, who was studying art in San Francisco, was coming home for Christmas after all.

Abby smiled. Her favorite sister home for Christmas. She hadn't seen Lizzie for almost a year. God, how she missed her.

A shard of homesickness pierced her heart. She closed her eyes and blinked back tears. When the moment passed, she continued reading.

Grandmama Maddy next reported on Little Falls's Harvest Festival, a country fair held every year on the third Saturday of October. This was the first year no Cooper horses were entered in the horse race in order to give disgruntled out-of-towners a chance to win. Some city slicker from New York had paid top dollar for every "quaint" quilt sewn by the quilting circle ladies. Helmut Blick won the pie-eating contest, and promptly got sick all over himself.

Grandmama's next entry brought Abby up short:

> As usual, the box lunch auction was the high-
> light of the Harvest Festival. You would have been
> so proud of your Kyle. When he saw that no one
> was bidding on poor Mary Dobbs's box lunch, he
> did. I know you wouldn't have minded. After all,
> you're far away in Chicago, and I'm sure you
> don't begrudge him some innocent fun.

Mary Dobbs, the mercantile owner's eighteen-year-old daughter, was as colorless as tap water, with pale, protruding eyes and a long nose. While the men in town wouldn't look twice at her homely face, their gazes always lingered on her ample bosom.

To the casual observer, Grandmama's comments

about Kyle glowed with approval. But Abby knew better. Her family made no bones about the fact that while they considered her an adult capable of choosing her own husband, they had reservations about this particular choice.

Her family's main objection was not the fact that Kyle ran One-Eyed Jack's, the local saloon, but that he employed several saloon girls well known for selling their favors upstairs. As Abby always pointed out to her family, Kyle didn't own the saloon, he only managed it, quite an accomplishment for a young man of twenty-two. His boss insisted on keeping the girls because of the added revenue. Kyle had promised Abby that as soon as they were married and he could afford to buy out his boss, he would get rid of the girls and turn One-Eyed Jack's into a more respectable establishment.

She opened Kyle's letter next. As she devoured every word, her fears and misgivings melted away like snow in sunlight. She grinned foolishly. He said he loved her. He said he missed her. He said he thought about her every second of the day, especially what had happened between them in the barn.

He said nothing about bidding on Mary Dobbs's box lunch. But then, why should he? It obviously meant nothing to him. He felt sorry for the plain wallflower, and just wanted to make her feel special for a few hours.

Grandmama of all people should have appreciated his generous gesture. She'd told her granddaughters often enough about the one Harvest Festival many years ago when no man had bid for *her* box lunch. She'd been as hurt and humiliated as Mary Dobbs. Like Kyle, Dr. Paul Wills, the man Grandmama later fell in love with and married, came to her rescue.

Abby looked over at Kyle's photograph on the nightstand. Her family would come around and accept Kyle once he gave Abby an engagement ring for Christmas. Then she and her fiancé would face her family and announce their intentions of marrying as soon as Abby graduated from veterinary school.

She leaned back and closed her eyes, reliving the last time they were together, the turning point in their relationship.

She had ridden into town on that late August day to visit Regina and her grandmother one more time before leaving for school. She was turning her horse loose in the small paddock behind her grandmother's house when Kyle appeared out of nowhere and drew her unprotesting into the nearby barn.

As soon as the door closed behind them and they were alone in the warm semidarkness that smelled of fresh straw and horse, Kyle took her in his arms and rained feverish, urgent kisses down her face.

"Do you have to go?" he moaned against her neck. "I'm going to miss you so much."

"You know I have to." She closed her eyes and let her head loll back. She loved the way his kisses made her feel all hot and fluttery inside, and sapped all resistance from her limbs. Her fingers dug into his broad, muscular shoulders. "It won't be long," she said breathlessly. "I'll be home for Christmas."

"It'll seem like forever," he said, steering her deeper into the barn, then pulling her down onto a pile of dusty, sweet-smelling straw.

She lay back, entwining her arms around him to hold him in place while his kisses grew deeper, more fervent. Her lips parted willingly, welcoming his claiming tongue and the accompanying blooming of her senses.

But, Abby felt there was something missing. She thought she should be feeling *more*.

Kyle pulled away. Abby's eyes flew open in shocked surprise when she felt the weight of his large, blunt-fingered hand on her breast.

Her cheeks burned with embarrassment, for he had never taken such liberties in the two years since they'd started courting. But she didn't push him away or protest. When his thumb rubbed her nipple, she felt more annoyance than pleasure.

"It feels good, doesn't it?" he whispered, his voice dark and thick and husky, his gaze limpid and intent. "Better than kissing."

She nodded, but actually, she preferred kissing.

Kyle stroked her other breast as he devoured her with his eyes. Now his fingers started undoing her shirt buttons. First one, then another. When Abby stiffened in surprise, he stopped.

"Maybe we shouldn't be doing this," he said, breathing hard as he leaned back on one elbow, his golden hair mussed invitingly by Abby's own hand. "Hard as it is, maybe we should wait until we're married."

She cradled his face in her hands and kissed him. "Maybe we should."

In the distance came the faint sound of Abby's grandmother calling her impatiently from the house.

"I'm sorry," Abby said, rising and brushing straw off the seat of her dungarees. "She'll kill me if she finds me in here."

"Well, maybe it's for the best." He surged to his feet and towered over her. He reached for her hand. "I can't control myself when I'm around you. There's no telling what might've happened."

They might have made love right here in the barn. Grandmama Maddy had called just in a nick of time.

In the short amount of time Abby had left, her family's demands managed to keep her and Kyle out of dark barns, so a relieved Abby left for Chicago still a virgin.

A loud knock on Abby's bedroom door jolted her out of her reverie. She blinked and looked around. She was no longer in her grandmother's barn back in Little Falls, letting Kyle take such liberties, but in her bedroom at Josie's.

Abby took several deep breaths to compose her runaway emotions, then folded her letter and slipped it back into its envelope.

When she opened the door, she found Bradshaw standing there, looking irate. "It's your cat, Miss Cooper. He snuck into my room again." He glanced at the healing scratches on the back of his hand. "I have no intention of touching him."

"I'm sorry," she said. "He must've gotten in when Josie was cleaning."

Bradshaw looked taken aback, as if bracing for an argument that never came.

Abby sailed past him and went to rescue Ulysses.

Later that evening, long after supper, Abby was about to close her textbooks and call it a night when the faint strains of piano music caught her attention.

She listened. The tune was a sprightly piano rag, a modern musical form much too complicated for Josie's basic skill. So who was playing? A guest?

She closed her textbooks and went downstairs. She stood unnoticed in the parlor doorway while James Bradshaw sat at the upright piano, his fingers coaxing some Scott Joplin out of the ivory keys. Josie sat on the sofa, swaying blissfully and tapping her toes to the infectious melody, while Ulysses perched behind her shoulder, listening with rapt feline intensity.

As Abby watched Bradshaw, it became increasingly obvious that the man had been playing since childhood. Someone had provided him with a piano and lessons. And he must have come from a privileged background that allowed a child ample time for study and practice.

The song ended with a flourish.

Josie rose, clapping enthusiastically. "Bravo, James. I haven't heard music like that since my dear departed Stanley and I went to the Exposition."

Bradshaw spun on the piano stool and started when he noticed Abby standing in the doorway.

"I quite agree with Josie," she said, walking into the parlor. "You're a man of many talents. Musician, veterinary student . . ."

Abby wondered what else Bradshaw was hiding. She was determined to find out.

He rose and crossed the parlor. Tonight he wore a black wool knitted sweater and black trousers instead of his customary suit and tie. With his dark hair and eyes, he seemed clothed in night, more a menace than a musician.

"Do you play, Miss Cooper?" he asked.

"No," she replied, fighting the urge to return to her room and lock the door. "Even if there had been someone to teach me, I wouldn't have had the time to practice. Too many chores on a horse farm."

Josie admonished Bradshaw to sit down and drink his cocoa before it got cold. Then she turned to Abby. "But your grandmother played." When Abby shook her head, Josie said, "When I was a little girl, I remember driving back to our farm in the evening with my father, and passing the boardinghouse. The downstairs windows were all lit up, and I could hear the sweetest piano music coming from inside. A fiddle, too. And singing.''

Abby lifted Ulysses' soft, warm heft into her arms. ''The elderly lady who ran the boardinghouse played the piano, and one of her other boarders accompanied her on his fiddle. Grandmama sang. She called them their musical evenings.''

''We could have our own musical evenings,'' Bradshaw said. ''That is, if Miss Cooper agreed to sing.''

''Sorry, but I can barely carry a tune,'' Abby replied, sitting on the sofa and settling her cat in her lap. She knew Bradshaw was trying to deflect her probing, personal questions by changing the subject. ''Where did you learn to play so well, Mr. Bradshaw?''

After Josie joined Abby on the sofa, Bradshaw took the chair opposite them and reached for his cup. He suddenly looked guarded. ''My mother taught me.''

When the conversation lagged pointedly, Josie poured Abby a cup of cocoa. ''And how is your grandmother?''

Abby brought Josie up to date on all the happenings in quiet Little Falls, while Bradshaw listened attentively.

Josie said, ''All is well with your young man?''

''Kyle is fine,'' Abby replied, her tone clipped. She didn't want to discuss the man she loved in front of Bradshaw.

Josie shook her head. ''I do wish he had another occupation, my dear. Running a saloon is—'' She caught herself before she could give offense, and shrugged apologetically.

Josie's father had been a drunkard, spending more time in One-Eyed Jack's than at the farm with his wife and four daughters. Now his eldest daughter wouldn't tolerate so much as a drop of sherry in her house.

"Kyle is a businessman who provides a service," Abby said, stroking Ulysses' thick, soft fur to calm herself and keep from saying something she'd later regret. "He doesn't force anyone to patronize the saloon, or drink."

A faint, angry blush tinged Josie's cheeks. "If the saloon didn't exist, men wouldn't have the opportunity to drink."

Abby sighed. "Let's not argue, shall we? Neither of us is about to change the other's mind."

Josie patted Abby's hand. "You know I so dislike arguing."

She became aware of Bradshaw studying them. "Do they have saloons where you come from?" she asked him.

He sipped his cocoa. "Of course."

"And where would that be?"

A faint smile played about his mouth. "Right here in Chicago."

Abby's stroking hand stilled on Ulysses' back. A native might know the location of abandoned factories. A native might know where to hire two thugs to abduct a woman.

She felt cold all over and moistened her dry lips. "If you're a native, why are you living here, instead of with your family?"

"I have no more family here. My parents are dead."

Both Abby and Josie offered their condolences.

"I find it odd that someone raised in the city would want to become a veterinarian," Abby said.

He drained his cup. "I spent several summers on a farm in England. Caring for the livestock was my responsibility, and I found I had a knack for it. That's when I decided to become a vet."

Ulysses stirred in Abby's lap and meowed, annoyed by the lack of attention. She resumed petting him. But her thoughts were on the man in black seated across from her.

Why had Bradshaw's parents sent him to summer in England? Abby's grandfather Wills had come from a wealthy Boston family, and his parents hadn't sent him to summer abroad.

"Would anyone like more cocoa?" Josie asked.

"If it wouldn't be too much trouble..." Bradshaw said.

"No trouble at all." Josie rose and headed for the kitchen, leaving Abby and Bradshaw alone.

He looked at Abby. "Why all the questions about my background?"

She shrugged. "Just making conversation."

"Or just curious?"

"A little of both." Under her stroking hand, Ulysses purred. "Josie is so trusting. She knows so little about you, yet she welcomes you into her home."

"I take it you're not as trusting."

"I'm afraid not."

He leaned forward, his dark stare intent. "You have nothing to fear from me."

But Abby wondered.

4

Abby hated city snow.

She hated the fierce, roaring wind that whistled through the eaves and rattled the windows just after midnight, sending her and Ulysses burrowing deeper under the warm covers. She hated waking up to the swirling, blinding whiteness collecting in windows, doorways, and alleys. She hated it even more when passing footsteps, wagon wheels, and hooves crisscrossed and churned the sugarcoated street into a quagmire of dirty brown muck.

She hated snow because her tormentors packed it into hard, cold missiles that bruised and stung. She suspected Shays and his cronies relished every snowfall as much as she dreaded them.

This morning, the storm had stopped long before Ulysses awoke her. Abby washed and dressed quickly, hoping to eat breakfast and disappear out the door before Bradshaw could join her. She liked walking to school alone, and had no desire for company. But there he was, sitting at the kitchen table. Waiting.

As they trudged off to class down barely shoveled

sidewalks, he stuck to Abby like a burr on a horse's mane. He said little beyond surface pleasantries about the storm and the ensuing cleanup until they reached the campus.

As they walked through the quadrangle, he stared at her, his dark eyes narrowing with a keen probing assessment. "What's the matter?"

"Nothing," she muttered, her wary gaze darting into every building's shadowed porte cochere for any sign of Shays and his cronies.

"Then why are you strung tighter than a piano wire?" he said. "Why do keep glancing over your shoulder as if Rockwell Shays is after you?"

The packed snow crunched beneath her boots with every cautious step. "Because he usually is."

"Don't tell me they throw snowballs at you." He snorted. "How childish."

Abby suspiciously eyed several students huddled together near the entrance to Walburg Hall. Hard to tell if they were discussing their classes or planning mayhem. They dispersed. She let out a soft sigh of relief when she saw they were not Shays and his cronies.

"Have you ever been hit in the head with a snowball, Mr. Bradshaw?" she asked.

"Once or twice."

"I can tell from your dismissive tone that you think it's rather insignificant. After all, children get into snowball fights all the time. What damage can one do?" Her gloved fingers absently touched her right cheekbone with its fine scar. "Last February, a snowball Shays threw hit me in the face perilously close to an eye, cutting my cheek. An inch higher, and I might've lost my sight."

She regretted telling him the moment the words were

out of her mouth. He might interpret her disclosure as a play for sympathy, which she didn't want or need.

"He shouldn't be allowed to get away with that," Bradshaw said. "Why haven't you complained to the dean about this harassment?"

"Oh, I have. On several occasions. And he's always condescending, treating me like a whining, complaining child. Once he even went so far as to say that I knew what I was getting into when I enrolled, so what did I expect?"

"Even after you were abducted?"

She nodded. "Dr. Hogg witnessed the snowball incident and forced officials to take action. When the dean called Shays into his office to answer the charges, the little weasel was the picture of offended innocence. He claimed that he hadn't meant any harm. A snowball fight was merely an expression of high spirits that got a little out of hand. Shays apologized to me, and the dean looked so pleased with himself."

Bradshaw shook his head.

She refrained from saying any more about Shays. After last night, when Bradshaw had been so reticent about his past, she still didn't trust him. Her only consolation was the fact that time was running out for Shays. If he intended to break her and force her out of college, he would have to act quickly.

They kept walking in silence.

James watched Abby look over her shoulder like a policeman on his beat. He felt sorry for her, though he knew evoking pity hadn't been her intention. He also admired her courage. Another woman who'd enrolled in the college hadn't lasted her first year after several masked men stopped her on her way home one night and stripped off her shirtwaist.

He knew Abby hadn't wanted him to accompany her to class this morning, but living in such close proximity to her in the boardinghouse made him feel responsible for her. How could he in good conscience stand by and watch Shays bother her when he had to face her over the dinner table every evening? Perhaps his mere presence would deter that bully.

Not that he wanted to come to blows. James had seen his share of violence and tried never to be a party to it in any form, even if its use was justified. He also didn't want to draw unwelcome attention to himself. If the truth about his father ever became public knowledge across campus, he'd never know peace.

He glanced at Abby, marching along resolutely, head held high and stubborn jaw set. He'd never met a woman of such strength and tenacity. She knew what she wanted, and she went after it.

Yet for all her ambition, he sensed a vulnerability that she tried so hard to hide beneath her icy armor.

Much as he hated to admit it, Miss Abigail Cooper was making it increasingly difficult for him to stay uninvolved.

Abby and Bradshaw arrived at the infectious diseases lab without incident.

Dr. Hogg gave them their assignments, then they all trooped over to the college's clinic, where anyone could bring his sick animal to be treated by the students for a nominal fee. They tended mostly cats, dogs, and cabbies' horses, with the occasional chicken or pet rabbit; for experience treating cattle, they traveled once a week to spend the day at the stockyards.

When they returned from the clinic with their collection of blood and body-fluid samples from the sick animals, each student went to his microscope to prepare slides and cultures. Then Dr. Hogg would ask for a diagnosis.

Abby, seated at her microscope, became so engrossed in her work that she relaxed her guard and failed to keep an eye on Shays seated at the opposite end of the laboratory. With the eagle-eyed professor walking around the room, Abby felt safe.

After retrieving a culture of chicken blood from a previous class, Abby put a sample under the microscope.

Dr. Hogg appeared at her side. "Will you tell the class what you've found, Miss Cooper?"

"Bacillus bipolaris septicus," she replied.

"And how did you come to that conclusion?"

"The bacteria stains intensely at the poles, but very little in the middle."

"And your diagnosis?"

"The chicken died of fowl cholera," she said.

Dr. Hogg addressed the rest of the class. "What would be our next course of action, gentlemen?"

Someone suggested immunization; Bradshaw was of the opinion that such a course of treatment would be too late, and any other chickens in the coop should be destroyed.

Hogg agreed, then walked around the room to each student, asking him to report on his findings. Then each of the students filed around the lab and took a turn looking at everyone else's slide, writing down their own diagnoses. Finally, after all the students made the rounds, they returned to their seats.

Next Dr. Hogg instructed them to make a drawing of their specimen.

When Abby looked through her microscope, she stared in shock. She swore aloud, her cheeks turning hot.

"What is it, Miss Cooper?" the professor demanded.

"Someone has switched slides on me," she said. "My bacillus has miraculous mutated."

"Mutated? Into what?"

"Spermatozoa."

Muffled guffaws and titters erupted among the men, save for Bradshaw, who shot a furious glance at Shays.

"Silence!" Dr. Hogg bellowed. "How many times have I told the lot of you that I will not have my classroom disrupted!"

The laughter dwindled and died.

"Since someone has gone to so much trouble to bring this specimen to my attention," Abby said to Dr. Hogg, "may I be allowed to assess its qualities?"

He nodded, his bristle brush mustache twitching with amusement.

Abby looked through her microscope, then at her classmates. "This specimen contains so very few sperm, gentlemen, I would have to say the animal is impotent, and would be an abysmal failure as a stud."

The class erupted into hoots of laughter. All except for Shays. He turned beet red.

"A very astute assessment," Dr. Hogg said. "Now, if we've all had our fun for the day, gentlemen and Miss Cooper, let's get back to work, shall we?"

Later, when Abby and Bradshaw left class together and strode down the hall, he said, "Didn't your mother ever tell you never to insult a man's . . . er, procreative abilities?"

Abby widened her eyes in feigned innocence. "That specimen was human? I thought it was from a bull or a stallion, and merely reported what I saw."

He shook his head as they started down the stairs.

"Be on your guard. Shays is going to want to make you pay for humiliating him like that."

Her lip curled. "I beg your pardon? He tried to humiliate me. What was I supposed to do? Ignore it? Let him get away with it? The only way to stop a bully is to stand up to him."

Bradshaw held open the door for her, and Abby stepped out into the blinding white of sun on snow. "You're the stubbornest woman I've ever met."

"I'm a scientist," she continued, squinting against the painful glare that stung her eyes. "Did he think I was going to shriek and swoon at the sight of dead sperm?"

"Obviously."

They had gotten halfway across the quadrangle, when a object came flying out of nowhere, striking Abby's hat with enough force to knock it off. With a startled cry, she bent to retrieve her hat, and another snowball went whizzing overhead, just missing her.

"God damn him," she muttered, straightening and turning to face her tormentors.

Suddenly a grim-faced Bradshaw stepped forward and pulled her against him, shielding her body with his own. Abby opened her mouth in protest as strong arms imprisoned her. She felt as though she were being sheltered behind a high, impenetrable stone wall. For one heart-stopping second, her senses registered only James Bradshaw.

Then she heard the dull thud-thud-thud of snowballs striking his shoulders and back. He flinched at each impact, but didn't release her.

"You all right?" he said, those onyx eyes filled with concern.

She took a deep breath to stop the trembling. "They only wounded my pride."

He turned and stepped away from Abby, revealing Shays, Evans, and Hendries standing several yards away, scooping up fresh snow for another round.

Then he looked at her, a devilish smile splitting his face. "Let's give them a taste of their own medicine."

Abby smiled back. She felt as though she were in Little Falls, she and her sister Lizzie allied against stuffy Regina. She watched as Bradshaw stripped off his gloves, scooped up some snow and formed a hard snowball, which he promptly threw, hitting a surprised Shays right in the chest.

"Take off your gloves," Bradshaw said. "The warmth from your hands will melt the surface snow and coat it with ice."

Abby sidestepped a snowball that Hendries threw, pulled off her gloves, and made her own snowball. "You've done this before, I see."

"Many times."

Abby threw her snowball back at Hendries. She missed.

"Put some muscle behind it, Miss Cooper," Bradshaw said, getting off another round, this time hitting Evans in the head. Evans looked astonished.

Abby formed another snowball and handed it to Bradshaw. "Be my guest."

He hurled the missile at Shays with bone-breaking force. Shays saw it coming and moved out of the way just in time. But his cronies had had enough. Both Evans and Hendries turned and started walking away.

"Get back here!" Shays yelled. "We're not through with them."

Before Shays had time to make another snowball, Bradshaw charged him, tackling him to the ground. Abby's hand flew to her mouth in horror, not knowing what to expect. To her surprise, all Bradshaw did was rub Shays's face in the snow.

Abby tugged her own gloves on her cold, wet hands and retrieved Bradshaw's from the ground. She walked over just as he was rising.

Breathing hard, Bradshaw looked down at the red-faced Shays. "Had enough?"

Shays nodded and hauled himself to his feet.

"Good. In the future maybe you'll think twice about throwing snowballs at me, or Miss Cooper."

"Can't you take a little joke, Bradshaw?" Shays dragged his coat sleeve over his wet red face and glared at Abby. "We were just having a little harmless fun."

"You've had enough harmless fun for the rest of the winter."

Shays turned and walked toward his cronies, who stood off a ways, waiting for him.

Abby handed Bradshaw his gloves. She felt awkward and embarrassed. She'd never expected him to come to her defense.

She took a deep breath and forced out a quick thank-you.

He raised one shoulder in a shrug. "I never could abide a bully."

As they headed back across the quadrangle, neither noticed Parson Brown standing in the shadows of a building's porte cochere, watching them.

James spotted the elusive Brown several days later.

He would have missed him if he hadn't stopped to buy a newspaper. As he tucked the *Chicago Tribune* under his arm and turned, he almost collided with the man.

The Parson stood stock-still. Only his dead gray eyes

widened briefly in resignation, like a trapped animal expecting the fatal bullet.

"Parson," James said, blocking his path. "Out of your usual neighborhood, aren't you?"

The Parson's lugubrious face registered as much emotion as a snake's. "You know me, Jimmy," he said in his rough, flat voice. "I get around."

"Let's talk," James said.

The Parson jammed his hands into his oversized coat, his breath barely vaporizing in the cold air. "Sure. Where?"

Since the Parson would surely draw attention at the tea shop on the corner, James said, "The alley by Kachinsky's."

They walked in silence. James shivered, and not from the cold. The Parson always had that effect on him.

When they reached their destination, James faced the Parson. "Why have you been following me? And don't deny it. I've seen you outside my boardinghouse."

"Your father wants to know where you are. When you checked out of the last place, he got worried. Told me to find you." He sniffed, and rubbed the tip of his nose with the back of his gloved hand. "Wasn't hard."

Not for a man of the Parson's assorted talents. Not for a man of Nick Flynn's wealth and powerful connections.

"I'm not trying to hide."

"Wouldn't have mattered if you were. I'd find you anyway."

"Now that you have found me, you can tell Nick that I'm fine. No need for him to worry." Or to send his bloodhound out tracking him.

"You can't blame a father for being concerned about his only son, Jimmy."

"I don't want anything from him," he said. "I never have, and he knows it." Not even his name. Especially that.

"That's the kind of man he is. Always worrying about his flesh and blood. Cuts him to the heart that you don't feel the same way about him."

James felt a churning in his gut. "An old song, Parson, and I refuse to play it."

The other man smiled, a thin grimace. "You always were the stubborn one, just like your mother."

"Tell him I'm fine," James said.

"You could tell him yourself. He wants you to come for Thanksgiving dinner."

"And if I don't?"

The Parson looked offended. "Nothing. He'd never hurt you. I'm surprised you could even think it."

James snorted in derision. "We both know what he's capable of."

"Yeah, but not to his own son."

The thought of enduring time in Nick's presence made James physically ill. "Give him my regrets. I plan to spend Thanksgiving with friends."

"What about Christmas?"

James raised one brow. "I didn't know Nick appointed you his social secretary."

A rare flicker of amusement warmed Brown's eyes for only a second, then died. "I just follow orders."

"I don't know what I'll be doing for Christmas." He intended to spend it like normal folk, in the boardinghouse, with Josie presiding over the festivities.

"He'll be disappointed."

Just as James was about to answer, Abigail Cooper walked past the alley on her way to the boardinghouse. He held his breath, praying she would look straight ahead and walk on without noticing him standing in the dark alley, talking to the Parson.

As luck would have it, she turned her head and looked down the alley. Her steps slowed with uncertainty when she spied James. When she noticed the Parson, she merely nodded and quickened her step.

When Parson Brown noticed Abigail Cooper, his sad features actually sparkled with interest, but then women were his weakness. "Looks like the lady knows you, Jimmy."

"We're fellow boarders."

"She's a beauty. All that dark hair and white skin. I'll bet she's hiding some body beneath that coat. She'd bring top dollar in one of your father's houses."

James fought down the impulse to grab the Parson by his lapels and fling him against the wall. Stronger, less intelligent men had died trying, but then, they weren't the only son of Nick Flynn. Instead, he clenched his jaw and counted to ten.

"She's not some whore," he said with deceptive calm, watching Abby cross the street and climb the boardinghouse steps. "And if anyone dares harm a hair on her head . . ."

The minute the words left his mouth, James knew he'd made a mistake. He'd just revealed a weakness for Nick to exploit. He could see the Parson taking the information and filing it away.

"Have feelings for her, do you?"

"Only the feelings one has for a friend," James replied, fighting to damp down his anger.

"She goes to that college of yours, doesn't she?"

No use denying it. James knew the Parson had been following him. "We're classmates."

The Parson wrinkled his long, sharp nose in distaste.

"Can't see a woman going to college. All they do is get married and have babies anyway. Don't need fancy book learning for that."

Not wanting to get into a philosophical discussion with Nick's henchman, James started walking away. "I've got to get back to my studies."

"See you around, Jimmy."

The words hung ominously on the air like a dirge.

Abby stood at the parlor window with a contented, purring Ulysses cradled in her arms and watched Bradshaw walk out of the alley. The man he'd been talking to headed down the street.

She hadn't expected to see Bradshaw standing in an alley, deep in conversation with that strange man. If the man was a friend, why hadn't Bradshaw invited him to the boardinghouse? Josie didn't object to callers. Perhaps Bradshaw didn't know.

Abby hadn't looked at the man for more than a few seconds, but he'd made an impression. His expression was about as cheerful as a bloodhound's, but the way he stared at Abby, as though undressing her with his eyes, gave her the chills.

He reminded her of the man who'd approached her at the train station when she first arrived in Chicago. Did she need a place to stay, he wanted to know? He could arrange the most comfortable, safe accommodations. Did she need a job? Chicago had plenty of employment opportunities for a lovely young lady like herself. He would be happy to arrange an interview for her with his boss.

Abby politely thanked him, but told him she was a college student and not seeking employment of any kind. And she already had a place to stay.

Then a furious Josie swept down on them like an avenging angel and threatened to report the man to the police. He quietly disappeared into the crowd. Abby later learned he was a "cadet," a man who frequented train stations, scouting out pretty, innocent country girls to work in the city's brothels.

Beyond his ingratiating smile, he had the same way of undressing her with his eyes.

Abby wondered how James Bradshaw knew such a man.

5

THREE DAYS BEFORE THANKSGIVING SO MANY ANI-
mals packed the school's veterinary clinic that Abby
wondered if an epidemic was sweeping the city. Most
of the four-legged patients were too sick and dispirited
to bark, meow, or neigh, so the clinic remained eerily
quiet, as if the lion had indeed lain down with the lamb.

Each student had more than a fair share of patients
that day. Some were overwhelmed. Others, like Abby
and Bradshaw, found the challenge exhilarating.

Still, Abby kept one cautious eye on Rockwell Shays.
He hadn't tried any fresh torments since Bradshaw
rubbed his face in snow, but Abby remained on guard.

While patching a sad-eyed little girl's marmalade cat,
which had been severely scratched and bitten in a vicious fight, Abby stood next to Bradshaw while he examined an old dog that moved so slowly and stiffly she
guessed it suffered from arthritis. Not only did he handle
the animal gently but he impressed Abby by speaking
soothingly to its owner, a shabbily dressed old lady
whose red-rimmed gaze clung to her pet.

When Abby finished her ministrations, she laid the cat

in a cushioned basket. The little girl rummaged in her coat pocket and pulled out a penny, which she handed to Abby.

"There's no charge today," she said, handing the coin back.

The little girl slipped the penny back in her pocket. "Billie and me thank you very much, miss." And she hurried off.

"Getting soft, Miss Cooper?" Bradshaw said. "You'll never make a living as a vet if you work for free."

Then he himself refused payment from the arthritic dog's owner, whose watery eyes overflowed as she thanked him for prescribing a special ointment.

He leaned forward, and in a conspiratorial whisper, said, "Just don't report me to the man in charge."

The old lady smiled and shuffled off.

Abby grinned triumphantly. "Getting soft, Bradshaw?"

"Button your lip, Miss Cooper."

As Abby washed her hands at the large communal sink, she said over her shoulder, "My grandmother often took eggs, chickens, jellies, and the occasional ham as payment for her veterinary services."

Bradshaw joined her to scrub his own hands. "That puts food on the table, but hardly shoes on your children's feet."

"I'll leave that up to my husband," she replied, "but who'll pay for *your* children's shoes?"

He grinned. "I'll manage."

Now, that comment piqued her curiosity. How did he expect to manage?

"I'll bet you're independently wealthy and have been keeping it a secret."

"You're right. I'm really a Rockefeller here in Chicago to study veterinary medicine incognito."

She could see that she wasn't going to pry any secrets out of him, so she just smiled. She dried her hands and watched Shays several tables away, examining a man's large, shaggy dog.

She caught Bradshaw's attention. "Look at Shays with that dog. He's so gentle and soothing, the animal isn't even nervous, though it's obviously in pain."

"Odd, isn't it, that the same man who possesses such compassion for dogs harasses you so mercilessly."

"Why does he do it?" she said in frustration. "What have I ever done to him?"

"Nothing, but that doesn't matter." Bradshaw hung up the towel. "Shays is the old-fashioned type who sees vet school, and any school for that matter, as a man's domain."

"Where women don't belong."

"Exactly."

"But just because I become a vet doesn't mean I'll be taking work away from him. I'll be practicing in Missouri, and Shays will be practicing somewhere else."

"It's a matter of principle to him," Bradshaw said. "Shays thinks women shouldn't be allowed into a man's world, and appeals to reason aren't going to change his mind."

Before Abby could comment, Professor Emerson came around and reassigned the students, sending Abby and Bradshaw to the far end of the clinic to treat horses.

Abby hated to be the one to tell young Tom Dawson that his horse had contracted glanders.

The symptoms couldn't be more obvious: a thick, glutinous discharge from one nostril, sores inside the nose, and a walnut-hard swollen gland between the branches of the lower jaw.

She wished she were mistaken, for the disease was highly contagious. Poor Star would have to be destroyed to keep from infecting healthy animals.

"How soon will it be before she gets better?" Dawson asked. He eked out a modest living as an independent light-freight driver, delivering parcels for various shops, and he had made it cold-water clear to Abby that his livelihood depended on Star's health.

Abby gave the horse a rueful pat on the forehead. Right now she wished she were anywhere else. She took a deep breath and said, "Mr. Dawson, I'm afraid Star has glanders."

"But that means—" Dawson's eyes widened, and he turned paper white. His jaw worked, but no sound came out. Finally he blurted, "No, you're wrong. Star has the catarrh, that's all. She'll be fine with some medicine and careful nursing."

Abby said nothing. Would she ever get over the sadness and regret of having to tell someone their animal would have to be put down?

Dawson's wild, desperate gaze darted around the clinic. "Where's another doctor?" he called out. "I want a *real* vet to look at her."

"I am a *real* vet," she replied coldly, bristling.

"I mean a *man*," he said. He looked her up and down contemptuously. "You're a woman. I shouldn't have even let you touch my Star. You don't know what you're talking about."

Hearing the raised voices, several of the students looked their way.

"I can assure you that I do indeed know what I'm talking about, Mr. Dawson." Abby felt her Irish temper ignite as it always did when she encountered prejudice based solely on her gender. "Whether you like it or not, your horse has glanders, and she will have to be put down."

He turned red. "I don't believe you. I want one of the others to look at her. One of the *men*."

"Fine," she snapped. "I'll get Professor Emerson."

Abby was so insulted and so furious with the ignorant, prejudiced Tom Dawson that she failed to exercise caution. She stepped back and bumped into a horse being led down the long corridor. The startled, skittish animal suddenly neighed in alarm, flung back his head and half reared. Surprise and alarm shot through Abby. She stepped away, but not fast enough.

As the horse descended, his right hoof lashed out and grazed Abby's right thigh.

She cried out as a searing pain shot down like a lightning bolt to her toes and up to her hip, momentarily unbalancing her. She fell to the floor with a grunt, managing to break her fall with her outstretched hands, which burned as they scraped the dirty, harsh cement.

Abby struggled to her knees, until she heard Bradshaw say from somewhere above her, "Don't move. Your leg may be broken."

"It's not," she replied in a quaking voice. "I could tell if it were. His hoof only grazed me."

Solicitous hands grasped her arms and gently pulled her to her feet. She stood there breathing hard, swaying and shaky, with her weight on her good left leg, while James Bradshaw held her.

"Are you sure you're all right?" he asked, his dark eyes grave with concern.

She nodded as she brushed bits of straw and dirt from

her skirt, aware that the other students were gathering around her, drawn by the commotion.

To her bewilderment, Bradshaw's expression suddenly shifted and darkened, turning so furious and fierce, she didn't recognize him. Then she realized his attention was directed, not at her, but over her shoulder.

"You did that on purpose, Shays," Bradshaw growled.

Abby half turned to see Shays holding the skittish horse's lead.

"It wasn't my fault," Shays snapped, stroking the horse's neck in an effort to calm him. "I was leading him to a stall when Miss Cooper suddenly came backing out into the corridor. She wasn't paying attention, and she bumped into the horse, scaring him. Before I could pull him in, he reared."

"You should've been keeping him on a shorter lead," Bradshaw retorted, his hands tightening on Abby's arms.

"You'd better keep that horse and all the others in the clinic away from Star," Abby said, her fear for the animals' health overriding her own pain. "She has glanders."

Dawson turned red, glared at her and swore. The other students exchanged knowing, alarmed looks. Shays shortened the horse's lead and quickly led him away.

Dr. Emerson moved through the clustered students straight to Star. "Are you sure it's glanders, Miss Cooper?"

"The symptoms are unmistakable, sir."

"Has her owner exhibited any symptoms?"

Glanders not only infected horses, but also humans.

"I haven't had time to question him about that."

While Emerson examined Star, he said to Abby, "Can you walk?"

She put her weight on her injured leg, and grimaced as a fresh wave of pain shot through her. She conquered it, and nodded.

"Mr. Bradshaw, will you escort her home and make sure she's examined by a doctor?"

"Of course."

"You needn't miss the rest of clinic," Abby said stiffly. "I can manage."

"Not this time," Bradshaw said. "I'm taking you back to the boardinghouse. Now."

Abby opened her mouth to protest, saw her own objections wither in the face of his overpowering determination, and said nothing.

Dr. Emerson addressed the rest of his class. "I'd suggest you gentlemen get back to work. This clinic doesn't close down just because someone gets injured by one of our patients. And we're going to have to keep this particularly nasty case of glanders from spreading."

"I can manage," Abby insisted as they walked slowly down the street, away from the campus.

Bradshaw gave her a skeptical look. "Then why are you limping? Why do you look as if you're about to faint?"

She took a deep breath and leaned more of her weight against the hard, unflinching support of his crooked arm. "You're walking too fast, that's all."

He shortened his stride until his own walk slowed to an accommodating shuffle. "Let me at least call us a cab."

"There aren't any around. If we wait for one, we'll be standing on a street corner for half the afternoon."

"There's a streetcar line two streets over."

"I'll be fine. Josie's isn't that far away."

"Several blocks can seem like a hundred miles when you're in pain." Bradshaw glanced down at her. "I know. You'll manage."

Each painful step sapped her strength further. Exertion dampened her forehead with a light film of sweat that made the cold afternoon air chill her face.

The pain finally stopped her.

Without warning, Bradshaw slipped his arm beneath her own and around her waist. Abby stiffened at the sudden familiarity of being tucked under his arm, of feeling his hard side pressed snugly against her.

"Don't pull away," he said. "Lean on me. More. Your whole weight. Take the pressure off that leg."

Abby did as he ordered. The pain lessened immediately. She closed her eyes and inhaled a deep, shaky breath.

Bradshaw's arm tightened around her waist, pulling her even closer. "Better?"

"Much."

"Now let's try walking. Lead with your left foot."

Abby leaned against Bradshaw and took a hesitant step. When she took another more assured step, before her right foot could strike the ground, Bradshaw startled her by effortlessly lifting her off her feet, and propelling her forward. Abby landed on her left foot, sparing her injured leg the shock.

"I feel like I'm running in the Founders' Day three-legged race," she muttered.

"What's Founders' Day?" Bradshaw asked. He helped her take another step, ignoring the curious stares of passersby. "And what's a three-legged race?"

Abby shook her head. "You city boys . . . In a three-legged race, the contestants pair up and tie one of their legs to their partner's." She took yet another step with

Bradshaw's help. "Instead of racing on four legs, they race on three."

"Sounds like fun."

"It is. And it requires a great deal of cooperation and coordination between the partners." She raised her brows. "I thought a big-city fellow like you would turn up your nose at such a simple country amusement."

"That'll teach you to make assumptions, Miss Cooper. You still haven't told me about Founders' Day."

Abby explained that Little Falls celebrated Founders' Day every May with a country fair. In October, they held a Harvest Festival, which was similar. Then she asked Bradshaw to stop so she could catch her breath.

He drew her out of the crush of pedestrians. "I've been to fairs in England," he said, "but never one in this country."

She remembered him saying something about having lived in England. She would have questioned him further if her thigh hadn't begun to throb afresh.

Bradshaw looked down at her, his brows knotted in concern. "You okay?"

Abby closed her eyes and took a deep breath, willing the pain to subside. She nodded.

"We still have three blocks to go."

Several blocks could stretch out into a hundred miles when viewed through a shimmering white haze of pain.

As Abby moved in tandem with Bradshaw like a pair of well-trained carriage horses, she ignored the curious and suspicious looks of passersby, some of whom gave them wide berth as if they were escapees from a mental asylum. But she couldn't ignore the strange reactions Bradshaw's closeness provoked in her.

Though they both wore heavy winter coats, Abby felt Bradshaw's arm as secure around her waist as a hoop around a barrel. Each time he lifted her, the shock of such close contact sent a faint blush rushing to her cheeks.

Two blocks later, she begged Bradshaw to stop.

"I can't take another step," she said, breathing hard.

"Then you shouldn't have to."

Before Abby could discern what he was doing, Bradshaw reached down, hooked one arm beneath her knees and the other around her waist. He swung her into his arms as if she weighed no more than a rag doll.

Abby cried out when he lifted her, and wrapped her arms instinctively around his neck.

"Sorry," he said, settling her in his arms, "but it's the only way we're going to get you home without an ambulance."

"The sooner, the better," she muttered between clenched teeth.

Abby rested her head on his shoulder and closed her eyes. She had thought that Kyle would be the first man to sweep her into his arms, carrying her, his bride, over the threshold of their new home. Not James Bradshaw, her academic rival, a man she barely knew and didn't even consider a friend.

And certainly not under these circumstances.

"We're almost there," he said.

Abby opened her eyes and studied Bradshaw's face, so close to hers she could have kissed his smooth, lean cheek if she wished. Which, she reminded herself hastily, she didn't. But he was as darkly attractive as her father, and though she felt a momentary pang of disloyalty for admitting it, much more handsome than Kyle. Still, looks weren't everything, even if Bradshaw did have a mouth Abby's Grandmama Maddy would have called a "sweet kissing mouth."

For the first time, she noticed that the pupils of his odd onyx eyes were surrounded by golden rays, like an eclipsed sun.

He smelled intriguing, too, a faint blend of cold wool, spicy shaving soap, and a clean, indefinable scent that must have been uniquely his own.

Abby blinked. She must be half out of her mind to be entertaining such personal speculation about James Bradshaw.

A minute later, they arrived at the foot of Josie's steps.

Abby thought Bradshaw would stop and let her down so she could grasp the iron railing and climb the steep stairs herself, but to her astonishment, he kept on going. She clasped his neck tighter, fearing that any minute he would falter and send both of them tumbling backward.

Even when they reached the top step, Bradshaw didn't release her. "Ring the doorbell."

"You can put me down now," she said. "I can manage."

Annoyance lit his dark eyes and he held her even tighter. "No, Miss Cooper, you cannot manage. You only think you can. The doorbell, if you please."

Abby reached out and cranked the doorbell.

Seconds later the door opened to reveal Josie, who stared wide-eyed and openmouthed. She swung the door wider and stepped aside so they could enter. "Oh, my . . . what happened?"

"A horse's hoof connected with my thigh," Abby explained as Bradshaw finally lowered her so gently she barely felt the shock when her feet touched the floor.

"Get a doctor," he ordered Josie, keeping one hand on Abby's elbow to steady her.

"It's just a bruise," she insisted. "A cold compress and some rest, and I'll be fine."

Josie exchanged looks with Bradshaw and reached for her coat. "I'll get Dr. Moore." Within seconds, she was bundled up and headed out the door.

"It's a conspiracy," Abby grumbled as Bradshaw helped her out of her heavy wool coat.

Relief and bone-deep weariness washed over her. Her leg hurt. She felt light-headed. She swayed on her feet.

Bradshaw slid his arm around her waist and steadied her. "I know you can manage, but I'll help you to your room anyway."

Hours later, Abby emerged from the oblivion of a sedated sleep to the warm tickle of Ulysses rubbing his face against her cheek. She was in her nightgown, lying in her bed, with the late afternoon sunlight bathing her bedroom in deep gold and blue shadows.

She drew her cat onto her lap and stroked him from head to tail, taking her usual comfort in his warmth and softness. Ulysses curled himself into a ball, closed his eyes, and purred.

Dr. Moore had examined Abby's thigh and told her she was damn lucky. She'd have an ugly, long-lasting bruise that would swell and knot and hurt like hell for a few days, but no bones were broken, and she'd recover.

She let out a sign of relief. If that horse had broken her leg, she would have had to drop out of college for the rest of the semester, possibly the rest of the year. Her studies would suffer. She wouldn't graduate with her class.

Now that she had time to think and reflect on the incident, she recalled Bradshaw saying something to

Rockwell Shays about how if he'd kept that horse on a shorter lead, it wouldn't have reared and injured Abby.

"Damn Shays!" she muttered. "That bastard led that horse right into me. He could've stopped him. He could've called out a warning."

Ulysses sensed her anger, for he raised his head and stared at her out of inscrutable green eyes.

"He wanted to hurt me," she told her cat. "Deliberately."

Ulysses continued to stare. If he had any thoughts on the subject of Rockwell Shays, he was keeping them to himself. Then he rose and climbed down Abby, stepping right on her bruise.

Abby gasped in pain and quickly lifted him off, setting him down on the coverlet. Ulysses jumped off the bed and trotted over to the window seat, where he proceeded to jump up onto the windowsill and its unobstructed view of the street below.

Rockwell Shays had set out to incapacitate her. And he'd almost succeeded.

What was he going to try next?

And then there was Tom Dawson, questioning her competency just because she was a woman. Even after Dr. Emerson, a "real" veterinarian of the accepted gender, had corroborated Abby's diagnosis of glanders, Dawson hadn't apologized to her for his insulting comments.

When she finally got her degree and opened her practice, would she face the same prejudice?

For the first time in three and a half years, Abby felt discouraged. She was tired of fighting. As terrified as she was when the two thugs abducted her, she had bounced back more determined than ever to graduate from veterinary school. Now she wondered if battling the Rockwell Shayses and Tom Dawsons of the world was worth the disrespect and abuse.

She stared at the ceiling. What if she did withdraw from college? Kyle would still marry her. Even though she wouldn't have a degree, she still knew enough about veterinary medicine to serve as Dr. Kendall's assistant. True, the work wouldn't be as challenging or satisfying, but she wouldn't have to worry about combining such a demanding career with raising a family.

Ulysses suddenly turned his head and gave her a look of pure feline disdain. Abby swore he could read her mind and was disturbed at the cowardly turn her thoughts were taking.

"Give up now?" he seemed to say. "After you've worked so hard?"

Her parents would be so disappointed. So would Grandmama Maddy. They would never say it to her face, but Abby would feel that she'd let down the women who'd come before her.

She had to make sure that didn't happen.

Abby flung back the coverlet, gritted her teeth, and got out of bed. She put on her kimono and reached for the cane that had once belonged to Josie's "dear, departed Stanley," and hobbled out of her bedroom, with Ulysses trotting at her heels.

She got as far as three steps from the bottom of the staircase before Bradshaw intercepted her.

"Where do you think you're going?" He looked up at her, his expression cold and furious. "The doctor told you to stay in bed."

"I've slept enough," she said. "Besides, I have a favor to ask of you."

He stared at her with Ulysses' unreadable intensity.

Then he extended his hand. "Come to the kitchen. I'll make you some tea."

She placed her hand in his, letting his warm, strong clasp take her weight as she negotiated the final three steps. Then he proferred his arm and escorted her into the kitchen.

"Where's Josie?" Abby asked once she sat down at the table.

"Visiting a friend in the apartments next door," Bradshaw replied, reaching for the teapot in the cupboard. He had changed into the casual black sweater that made him look more like a dock worker than a student. "Now, what's this about a favor?"

"Since I won't be able to attend classes tomorrow, may I borrow your notes?"

"Of course." He grinned. "That must've cost you."

Abby's cheeks turned pink. "I don't like asking for favors."

"I know." He filled the kettle with water. "You don't need favors. You can manage just fine on your own."

"Usually. But that's neither here nor there." She moistened her dry lips. "Did you see Shays deliberately lead that horse into me?"

He leaned back against the edge of the counter and folded his arms. "If Shays had kept that horse on a shorter lead, he could've prevented the animal from rearing and striking you. But that's only my opinion. And it would be hard to prove."

"So I'd be wasting my time if I complained to the dean."

"I doubt if he'd do anything without solid proof."

Abby groaned. "I thought I'd finally be able to get Shays off my back."

"Without proof, that'll be difficult," Bradshaw said.

"If Kyle or my father were here, they'd make sure Shays left me alone." She smiled. "He'd get the message loud and clear."

Bradshaw raised his brows. "They'd resort to violence?"

"If they had to," she replied coolly. "The good men of Little Falls don't hold with mistreating women."

"Neither do I."

6

"YOUR FATHER WANTS TO KNOW IF YOU'VE changed your mind about joining him for Thanksgiving dinner."

James glanced over at the Parson, who had suddenly materialized by his side, as noiseless as a ghost. At least Brown had waited until James left the campus so they wouldn't be seen together.

"I haven't changed my mind," James said, not breaking stride as he looked into the other man's soulless eyes. "I'm spending Thanksgiving at the boarding-house."

Josie had promised him a feast he'd never forget complete with turkey, chestnut-and-sausage stuffing, creamed onions, and cranberry sauce. More than the food, he was looking forward to the company. Josie had generously welcomed him into her home and treated him like family. Even the cool Miss Cooper had been thawing toward him, especially after he'd assisted her when she'd been injured. Perhaps the three of them could create the illusion of family, if only for a day.

The Parson's hangdog expression didn't alter. "He's going to be real disappointed, Jimmy."

James raised a brow. "Since when? Thanksgiving's never meant anything to Nick Flynn. Just another day." Another day to tend to his numerous lucrative "business" interests.

Bitter memories caught him unawares, recollections of Thanksgivings past spent sitting with only his perfumed, bejewelled mother at one end of the mile-long mahogany table in the formal dining room, waiting for the father who never came. Mother would break the awkward, interminable silence with forced chatter that echoed through the cavernous room. Then she'd bow her head and say grace, giving thanks for a long list of material comforts Nick Flynn provided as a way of instilling gratitude in James. The litany of words without substance had always struck him as a mockery. Eventually the butler would stand in for the absent head of the household and carve the turkey.

"The boss's getting along in years," the Parson said, surprising James with such an uncharacteristic philosophical turn. "A man gets reflective when he gets older. He starts thinking about the mistakes he's made. About mending fences."

"Mending fences?" James snorted in derision. "Nick?"

Brown fell silent. He knew better than to waste his time trying to change James's mind.

"What happened to your lady friend?" Brown asked.

A trickle of alarm crept down James's spine. The less Parson Brown knew about Abigail Cooper, the better. "What do you mean?"

"I saw you carrying her down the street." The Parson's thin, bloodless lips stretched into a mirthless grimace. "I didn't think you were kidnapping her."

He may have seen James, but James hadn't seen him.

Of course, he'd literally had his hands full at the time, and he thought Nick's henchman had left the neighborhood. He should have known better.

"She had an accident at the clinic," James said. Best to tell the truth. The Parson would find out sooner or later if he was lying. "A horse injured her leg."

A flicker of what could have been surprise passed across Brown's impassive face. "Did the horse hurt her bad? I noticed a doctor going into your house."

"She's fine," James said. "She'll be back on her feet in no time."

She'd attempted to dress for school this morning, but the pain had overwhelmed her, sending her back to bed.

"Glad to hear it wasn't anything serious."

James resented the Parson's spying, but he knew from long experience that he couldn't stop it. Parson Brown was merely following orders. He always followed orders with the tenacious singlemindedness of a bulldog. That's why he'd survived so long in Nick's violent world.

Following the sidewalk's track of dirty, packed snow down the street, James felt another stirring of uneasiness. Nick Flynn was creeping closer and closer like a winter fog, trying to insinuate himself into his estranged son's life.

A whisper of cold that had nothing to do with winter weather brushed the back of James's neck. He didn't shiver. He accepted it as a warning.

When they reached the tea shop on the corner, Brown stopped. "What about this Rockwell Shays?"

"He's one of my classmates," James said, dismissing Shays with a casual shrug. "Why?"

Parson sniffed and dragged the tip of his nose across his coat sleeve. "I was having a beer in a bar by the college when Shays and two of his friends came in. They started talking. Lucky for you, I've got big ears.''

James glanced at his watch, more to dismiss the Parson than to check the time. ''This is all very interesting, but—''

''He was saying nasty things about you, Jimmy. And your lady friend.'' Brown gave him a hard, unblinking stare. ''Nick wouldn't like somebody threatening his kid.''

Talking to Brown was as good as whispering in Nick's ear, so James said, ''Shays is a blowhard. He makes meaningless threats, and nothing comes of them.'' A lie, but he had to do something to throw both Nick and his bulldog off the track.

''I know when a man means business,'' Parson said.

James stepped forward until he was so close to the Parson, he could see the enlarged pores on the man's red nose. ''Leave Shays alone. I can take care of myself.''

''Not as well as I can.''

James envisioned Shays lying dead in an alley with a knife stuck between his ribs, or his throat slit from ear to ear. Even Shays didn't deserve such a fate. ''I said, leave Shays alone.''

''Or—?''

Both of them knew James couldn't stop the Parson from harming Shays if Nick Flynn ordered it.

''I'll fight you, if I have to,'' James said evenly. He looked the Parson up and down. ''Who knows? I might even take you.''

Parson Brown grinned with genuine amusement. ''Don't get hot under the collar, kid. It'll never come to that, and you know it.''

''Just so we understand each other.''

Brown nodded.

They always had.

The Parson stepped back. A sudden gust of wind caught his long, black coat so that it flapped and billowed out around him, turning him into an ominous winged predator poised for flight.

"You're too soft, Jimmy." He shook his head. "Hard to believe you're Nick Flynn's son."

James smiled. "I'll take that as a compliment."

The Parson grunted. "Watch out for Shays. He's a bad one."

With a curt nod, Brown turned and walked back the way he'd come. In the blink of an eye, the Parson blended in with the other pedestrians until he vanished.

When James came to the boardinghouse steps, he paused, then kept on walking. He couldn't face the women just yet. He needed time to calm down, to control his anger.

Why couldn't Nick stay out of his life? He knew James wanted nothing to do with him, and with good reason. Yet he persisted in reappearing when James least expected it.

James had thought he was finally rid of the man he couldn't bear referring to as his father. Ever since he'd started college, he hadn't seen hide nor hair of Nick. No invitations to Thanksgiving dinner, no lavish Christmas gifts delivered anonymously to wherever James was living. Just a deposit every January 2 in James's bank account to cover college expenses following the letter of their agreement.

Once James graduated in June and found himself a veterinary practice in the country, as far away from Chicago as possible, he would leave the past behind and start a quiet, peaceful new life.

"Why can't he just leave me alone?" James muttered to himself, causing several passersby to stare. "I'm not like him. I never will be."

He had to walk several blocks before he finally spent his anger. Then he turned and marched back to the boardinghouse.

The minute he opened the front door and stepped inside the foyer, the homey, enticing aromas of cinnamon and baking pies surrounded him. Memories of the huge kitchen in his father's Prairie Avenue mansion leaped unbidden to his mind. The temperamental French chef's rich, elaborate creations calculated to impress couldn't hold a candle to Josie's simpler stick-to-your-ribs fare.

James hung up his coat and was about to go to the kitchen to investigate the tantalizing aromas when he passed the parlor door and noticed Abigail dozing in a chair by the window.

She had propped a pillow behind her head, rested her arms on the chair's wooden ones, and put her feet up on an ottoman, another pillow beneath her knees to elevate them. Her sleeping cat lay stretched along her wrinkled brown skirt from its waist to the knees, unmindful of his mistress's injured leg. Selfish cat, hogging all the warm afternoon sunlight beaming through the window.

James stepped quietly into the parlor. Neither the woman nor her cat stirred. James suspected Ulysses had detected his presence the minute he opened the door, but with typical feline selfishness, decided that James was unworthy of disturbing his afternoon nap.

Nick had always surrounded himself with stunning women who could make a man hot and hard with one sultry glance. But James still thought Abigail Cooper was one of the most beautiful women he'd ever seen.

She was more than the seductive cloud of dark Gibson girl hair, smooth, flawless white skin, and slender, curving body that had caught the Parson's expert eye. She possessed an inner goodness that added a certain radiance unmatched in more experienced women.

Watching her doze, her rosy lips parted slightly, her thick dark lashes two crescents against her cheeks, James felt an overwhelming urge to protect her. Being abducted had taught the sheltered farm girl from Little Falls, Missouri, about the darkness and violence that prowled the edges of everyday existence. Such an experience always left scars. Always.

James knew too much about scars.

Abigail stirred. She opened her sleepy blue eyes, and noticed him standing there. She sat up abruptly, flinched in pain, and dislodged Ulysses. The cat leaped from her lap to land lightly on the floor, where he sat flicking his tail.

She stifled a yawn with the back of her hand. "Mr. Bradshaw."

He raised a mocking brow. "Still so formal, my dear Miss Cooper, after all we've been through together? A snowball fight, my carrying you in my arms . . ."

He wanted her to call him James. Needed to hear her say it in her soft, sweet voice.

"Mr. Bradshaw—"

"If you won't call me James, I won't share today's notes with you."

Irritated sparks turned her blue eyes ocean green. "That's blackmail!"

He grinned. "I know."

The cat, disgusted with their exchange, rose and sauntered out of the parlor, headed, no doubt, for James's room and that intriguing mousehole.

Abigail stared at him in silence. He could almost see her mentally weighing her need for the notes with her need for keeping him at arm's length.

"All right, you win," she said. "James it is, if you'll call me Abby."

"My pleasure." He knelt down to pick up the cane she'd left lying on the floor by her chair. "How's your leg?"

"Black and blue and very sore." She swung her legs off the ottoman and groaned.

He looked down at her. "Is there something I can do to help you?"

"Just let me sit here quietly for a minute," she said, taking a deep breath, "and the pain will pass."

James set his notebooks down on a nearby table. "I wonder what Josie's baking? Smells delicious."

Abby cast a guilty glance at the door. "She's making pies for Thanksgiving, and I promised to help her roll out the crusts. But then I fell asleep."

James wondered fleetingly if any of Nick Flynn's women had ever rolled out a pie crust. Somehow he doubted it. Their skills were not of the domestic variety.

"Under the circumstances, I think Josie will excuse you." He glanced at his books. "Why don't you just sit right there, and I'll go over today's notes with you."

Abby gave him a long, speculative look. "Why are you doing this?"

He pulled another chair over and sat down across from her. "Doing what?"

"Sharing your notes with me. If you didn't, I'd fall behind and you'd be one step closer to being valedictorian."

Outrage swamped him. After the times he'd defended her against Rockwell Shays, after all he'd done to prove his trustworthiness, how could she could even think he'd do something so petty and calculating?

James rose and glared down at her. "Get your damn notes from someone else."

He turned and started for the parlor door.

"James, wait. Please." Her plea was followed by a sharp cry.

He turned to see that Abby had struggled to her feet, obviously intending to come after him. She hadn't gotten very far. She was grasping the back of her chair to steady herself. Her lips were pursed, and she looked about ready to collapse.

He was at her side in three strides. "What in the hell are you trying to do?" he said gruffly. "Fall and cripple yourself?"

He slipped his arm around her waist to lower her gently back into her chair.

"I'm sorry," she said. "That was mean, and you didn't deserve it."

"No, I didn't." When she was settled again and her color returned, he returned to his chair and opened his notebook. "If I'm going to be valedictorian, it'll be because I earned it, not by default."

She studied him with an unnerving thoroughness. Then she gave an almost imperceptible nod as if she'd just arrived at a monumentous decision.

"You're an honorable man, James Bradshaw," she said softly.

An honorable man. Nothing like Nick Flynn.

He looked at her. Was the Ice Maiden beginning to thaw? She actually appeared to be at ease with him, rather than suspicious.

"Now," he began, "would you like to hear what Professor Hogg had to say about pneumonia?"

• • •

On Thanksgiving Day at one o'clock in the afternoon, Abby steadied herself by holding on to the back of a chair and surveyed the dining room table. Fragrant steam rose from dishes of creamed onions and mashed potatoes. Hot crusty rolls baked just that morning lay nestled in a napkin-lined basket. Green beans, stuffing, and cranberry sauce completed their feast.

"I think we're just about ready to eat," she said.

As if on cue, Ulysses came trotting into the dining room, leaped on Abby's chair, and licked his chops.

"Oh, no, you don't." Abby shooed him away. "If you think there's anything here for you, you're sadly mistaken."

James, who was pouring root beer into Josie's Chicago Exposition souvenir wineglasses, raised a mocking brow. "Your cat won't be joining us at the table?"

"As much as I love this reprobate," she said, "I do not agree with letting animals dine at the table."

Ulysses sauntered over to a nearby corner where he would wait patiently for the tidbits he knew would come his way.

After James finished pouring, he assisted Abby to her seat at his right. At least her leg didn't hurt as much today, and she was able to get around without limping too badly.

Footsteps coming from the kitchen heralded the arrival of Josie bearing the turkey on a large oval platter.

James rushed to take it from her and bring the turkey to his place at the head of the small table, for Josie had asked him to do the honors and carve.

"Josie, you've outdone yourself," Abby said, admiring the bird's glistening, golden brown perfection.

Josie smiled and patted her hair's coronet. "I do think so."

James picked up the carving knife. "I've never carved a turkey before, so I can't guarantee the results."

"Think of it as performing surgery," Abby said without cracking a smile.

James grinned. "Amputating a turkey's leg?"

"Exactly."

Abby thought he did a credible job of wielding the carving knife when he laid several thin slices of white turkey breast on her plate and passed it over to her.

Once all the side dishes had been passed, and everyone's plate was full, Josie looked around the table. "Why don't we each evoke the Lord's blessing on those members of our families who can't be with us today?" She bowed her head and folded her hands.

Abby and James followed suit.

"Dear Lord," Josie began, "bless our bounty, and those we love who are far away. Please bless my sisters, Rose, Clara, and Melinda, their husbands and children." Josie's voice quivered with deep emotion. "And keep our little Bitsy at your side in heaven. Amen."

Abby took a deep breath. "Dear Lord, bless Kyle, my parents, and my sisters. Give strength to Grandmama Maddy, on this, her first Thanksgiving without Grandpapa Paul, and to my Grandpapa Jace, who lost Grandmama Clementine this year." She felt the sting of tears, and her lower lip trembled. But she managed a hasty, "Amen."

She waited for James to start.

Silence.

Abby was just about to prod him with a warning look, when he said, "May the good Lord bless and keep my late mother. Amen."

He had said his parents were dead, but why hadn't he mentioned his deceased father? Abby supposed he had his reasons.

Josie and Abby echoed his amen, then James raised his wineglass. "I'd like to propose a toast."

The women raised their glasses.

"To good friends," he said, his dark eyes holding Abby's as the three glasses came together with a loud clink. "And may this house always know great joy."

"To good friends," she and Josie said in unison. "And great joy."

Then they all dug in.

As Abby ate and smuggled a few tasty morsels of turkey to Ulysses, her thoughts kept straying back to James and his terse, succinct evocation. Ever since he'd moved into the boardinghouse, she'd been trying to learn more about the secretive, mysterious James Bradshaw. She'd only learned that he was a native Chicagoan, and unlike Abby and Josie, he had no siblings.

Abby sipped her root beer and listened to Josie tell James about her sisters. She decided that she may have misjudged James. After years of harassment by Shays, she'd found it difficult to trust any of the male students. But James had recently defended her against Shays on more than one occasion. If he were truly out to sabotage her studies, he wouldn't have lent her his notes.

Josie's voice suddenly turned wistful. "We didn't have much of Thanksgiving when I was a little girl living in Little Falls. We were dirt poor because my father was a drunkard who couldn't make a go of that farm to save his life. We never had a turkey for Thanksgiving. He'd usually kill one of the chickens, and that would have to do."

James refilled Josie's glass. "But that all changed when you moved to Chicago, didn't it?"

Her face brightened at the memory. "My mother's sister had married well, and lived in a beautiful, big house. Two girls each shared a bedroom." She shook her head. "In Little Falls, my whole family of seven shared a two-room cabin."

Abby asked James to pass the creamed onions. As she spooned them on her plate, she said, "What I remember most about Thanksgiving when I was a child is having to sit with my sisters at a special children's table in the kitchen, while all the grown-ups got to sit at the dining room table."

James grinned. "Such injustice."

"I thought it was," Abby retorted. "Then when we turned twelve, we were allowed to join the adults. I felt like such a grown-up."

While James carved second helpings of turkey, Josie said, "What do you remember most about your childhood Thanksgivings, James?"

Abby held her breath and busied herself feeding another scrap to her cat.

"What I remember most about my childhood Thanksgivings," he said lightly, "is that my mother and I spent them dining alone. My father's business frequently took him away from home."

"On a holiday?" Josie asked in patent disbelief. Holidays were sacred to her.

"Holidays didn't matter to my father."

Abby caught the faint, underlying bitterness in his voice, and when Josie opened her mouth, Abby could tell it was to ask James another personal question. She gave Josie a pointed warning glance. Her landlady fell silent.

They made small talk during the rest of the meal, and then Josie served coffee and dessert. When they finished they retired to the parlor, where James played the piano late into the afternoon.

A sleepy, overstuffed Josie stifled a yawn, rose, and announced that she was going upstairs to nap. At the parlor door, she paused and turned.

"By the way," she began, "my sister Rose has invited me to spend Christmas with her and her family in Evanston. Abby, I know you'll be going to Little Falls." She looked at James. "If you don't have anywhere to go for Christmas, you're welcome to stay here, though there'll be no one to cook for you."

"And you'll have to endure Ulysses' company," Abby said. "I usually leave him here for the holidays, and Josie's friend Mrs. Gray comes in to feed him."

James swung around on the piano stool. "I'll be fine here by myself. Chicago has no shortage of restaurants. And I'll be happy to feed Ulysses, as long as he keeps out of my room."

The thought that James had nowhere to go for Christmas tugged at Abby's heartstrings.

Later she went upstairs to her room and was so absorbed in the letter she was writing to her mother that she failed to hear James leave the boardinghouse.

7

THE LAST VESTIGES OF DAYLIGHT WERE MELTING into twilight, shadowing the ruffled surface of Lake Michigan a deep cobalt blue by the time James arrived at his father's house on Lake Shore Drive, Chicago's exclusive Gold Coast.

No crowded apartment buildings rubbed shoulders with the spacious mansions, and no butcher shops spoiled the views from these parlor windows.

James stood on the sidewalk, his feet braced against the brisk wind whipping around him, numbing his face, and stared at his former home. Not *home,* he corrected himself. The *house* where he and his mother had once lived. A subtle, but important, distinction in James's mind. He'd never thought of this cold gray granite pile as anything as warm and welcoming as a home.

The dominant impression Nick Flynn's Romanesque-style mansion created in the casual observer was of an impregnable fortress ready to withstand the longest siege. The wrought-iron fence guarding the property like a row of tall, sharp spears first contributed to the effect. Next came the deeply recessed porches, where anyone could watch from the shadows without being seen from the street. Finally the imposing round tower topped by a conical roof and taking up the house's entire left corner looked as though it could harbor medieval soldiers ready to rain arrows and boiling oil down upon hapless pedestrians. In actuality, James remembered that Nick liked to go up to the tower's top unenclosed porch after dinner and do nothing more threatening than smoke a fine Havana cigar and gaze out over the lake like an English lord overseeing his domain.

James shook his head at his own fancies as he opened the gate and walked up the smooth stone steps. If anyone ever laid siege to Nick Flynn's private domain, it would be the Chicago police.

James walked through the arched entrance and hesitated, his hand poised to ring the bell. He still had time to turn around and return to the boardinghouse.

He twisted the bell savagely. He'd never shied away from a confrontation with Nick, and he wasn't about to start now.

Several seconds passed before the door swung open.

"Good evening, Gardiner," James said to the butler. He waited, never taking his welcome for granted.

Gardiner smiled. "Why, Mr. James . . ." He swung open the door. "Do come in."

James stepped into the tower's warm, round foyer, relieved to leave the cold, blustery afternoon behind.

When Gardiner offered to take James's coat, he divested himself of his hat and gloves as well, then followed the butler into the main hall. His gaze veered automatically to the staircase landing and the dramatic life-size portrait of his mother.

James blinked hard. His mother's portrait had been hung low, and at such an angle that in the hall's soft, deeply shadowed light, from where James was standing, he could easily imagine that his mother was alive and poised on the landing, giving guests and servants alike the opportunity to admire her before she made her grand entrance.

The favorite society artist of the 1890s, John Singer Sargent had come to Chicago expressly to paint Lucille Bradshaw's portrait for an exorbitant commission. When Nick saw the results, he considered his money well spent. The artist had successfully captured not only the former actress's strong-willed, magnetic presence, but also her humor and warmth, qualities much more elusive and difficult to reproduce with paint and brush than her striking dark-haired, dark-eyed physical beauty.

"The master's in his study," Gardiner said, distracting him. "Would you prefer to go there directly, or shall I announce you?"

"Announce me."

No sooner did the butler stride off and disappear through the main doorway than a low, warning growl sounded from another arched entrance to the right.

James turned to see a large fawn-colored mastiff standing there at attention and regarding him as if he were a meaty ham bone.

But James and Moriarty, whom Nick had named after Sherlock Holmes's nemesis, were old friends.

"Moriarty," he said sharply. "Hug!"

The mastiff's black, wrinkled face brightened at the familiar command, and his tail whipped back and forth like a metronome. Then he bounded across the hall with all the unbridled enthusiasm of a puppy one quarter his size. Whimpering excitedly, the dog slid to a stop at James's feet. James barely had enough time to brace himself before Moriarty stood on his hind legs and rested his long forelegs against James.

James wrapped his arms around the big dog and hugged him. "Atta boy, you big lug."

He stepped back and petted Moriarty's morose face with its silly doggy grin. He examined the dog's clear brown eyes and lifted his floppy jowls to examine his strong white teeth. Relieved that the seven-year-old still looked healthy and fit, James rubbed Moriarty's deep, powerful chest. "Kiss."

The mastiff licked his cheek with such relish that James laughed and staggered back from the onslaught, pushing the dog away. Moriarty wasn't offended. When all four paws landed back on the floor, he nudged James's hand with his broad head, indicating his desire for more attention. James obliged by petting him and repeatedly reassuring Moriarty that he was a good dog.

Gardiner reappeared to tell James that his father would see him now. Nicholas Flynn never came out to the hall to greet anyone; everyone went to him.

James told Moriarty to lie down, then went for his audience.

When James reached the study's imposing double doors, he stopped. He took several deep breaths and mentally willed himself behind an impenetrable stone wall. Then he knocked and waited until he heard a cultured voice invite him to enter.

James opened the doors and strode into the study as if he owned it. He knew from painful past experience that Nicholas Flynn drew strength from his opponent's weakness.

Nick was dressed in white tie today, standing by the crackling fire, one arm draped negligently along the mantel, a studied picture of command and power.

However, he'd lost the power to intimidate James. Anger him, yes. Inspire hatred and bitter resentment, absolutely. But not intimidate.

"You're late," Nick said, his ice blue gaze annoyed. "Thanksgiving dinner was hours ago."

"I told the Parson to tell you that I wasn't coming for dinner," James said.

Unlike Parson Brown, who looked as frightening and unprincipled as the thug he was, Nicholas Flynn presented the picture of refinement, fitting in perfectly with the study's warm oak-paneled walls, and the pair of inviting oxblood leather Chesterfield sofas positioned cozily near the fireplace. Not quite as tall as his son, he was still lean and strong for his fifty-five years. Two swathes of white hair sweeping away from his temples only made him look more distinguished, like some blue-blooded banker. And he certainly knew how to use his handsome, craggy features to disarm.

But James knew that the only part of the room that honestly reflected Nick's true nature were the instruments of death and destruction—a medieval battle ax, a jeweled Renaissance dagger, a pair of English dueling pistols, and two Civil War swords, one Union and one Confederate—displayed on the farthest wall.

"Then why are you here?" Nick inquired politely in his smooth, well-trained voice.

"To tell you to call off the Parson and keep out of my life."

Nick walked over to a small table, picked up a cut-glass decanter and raised an inquiring brow at James. When James shook his head, his father shrugged, removed the stopper, and poured himself a glass of the finest imported scotch.

Nick raised his glass. "To your future." He took a

sip, savored it like the gentleman he wasn't, then carried his drink over to one of the sofas. "Have a seat. Make yourself comfortable."

"I'd rather stand."

Nick shrugged and sat down, the butter-soft leather barely creaking under his weight. "Suit yourself." He studied James for an endless moment. "Whether you want to admit it or not, my boy, I'm still your father. You're still my flesh and blood." He took another sip. "With her dying breath, your mother made me promise to always look after you."

"I'm a grown man," James snapped. "I can damn well take care of myself."

"I wouldn't expect any less of my son."

"Then call off your bulldog."

Nick looked away. "The Parson tells me there's a man at your college who's been giving you trouble."

"Not me," James said. "A friend of mine."

"Ah, yes. Miss Abigail Cooper, the only woman student in the Chicago Veterinary College. She also lives at your boardinghouse."

James wasn't surprised at the extent of Nick's knowledge, but forced himself to remain cool. "What else do you know about her?"

Nick sipped his scotch, his urbane expression turning smug. "Everything. Except whether you're sleeping with her." He smiled. "Are you?"

"None of your business."

"Why aren't you? The Parson says she's a stunning woman. Dark hair, blue eyes. A graceful, womanly figure pleasing to a man. Surely you can't spend all your time studying."

"Leave her alone, Nick," James said, in a quiet, deadly voice.

"Or—?"

"Or I'll beat you like I did when I was eighteen. You're older and slower now, so you'll really feel it."

A triumphant grin lit Nick's lean face. "A threat. Now you sound just like your old man. Looks like you've got some of Nick Flynn's blood in you after all."

Damn him! He set me up and I walked right into it. And all because I want him to leave Abby alone.

James's rising temper started a fissure in his mental wall. He fought to seal the crack before it spread, destroying the wall and leaving James defenseless.

"You're not exactly the kind of father a son can be proud of," he said. "You're a common criminal, Nick. You steal. You extort. You kill."

"I haven't killed anyone in a long time. And I resent being called common."

The indignation in Nick's voice almost made James laugh. He felt his rigid self-control slipping away. He propped his hands on the low back of the other sofa and leaned forward. "Don't you understand? I'm ashamed of you. I don't want anyone at college to know that one of the most notorious vice kings of Chicago is my father."

"I've never claimed to be a saint, and I don't make excuses for my life. I did what I had to do to survive." Nick drained his glass. "But I am your father. It hurts me deeply to see you filled with so much bitterness and hatred."

James straightened and walked over to the fireplace. He grasped the mantel edge and stared down into the dancing, crackling flames. He'd worked so hard to keep his life of healing animals and his father's life of crime separate. He didn't know what he'd do if anyone learned of his shameful background.

What would an honest, decent woman like Josie think, she whose parents had been murdered by men as lawless as James's father? Would she evict him? Or Abby, who'd already suspected him of being in league with Shays to drive her out of school? Would she recoil in horror?

He turned and faced Nick. Threats hadn't worked. Perhaps swallowing his pride and begging would. "Please stay out of my life."

Nick raised his flaring brows. "A first. My son actually *asking* me for something."

"Please."

"I promised your mother I'd always look after you."

So much for begging.

Nick's expression suddenly grew wistful. "I loved her, you know. And she loved me."

"Lord knows why," James scoffed. "She was the toast of New York, with a stellar dramatic career ahead of her. She could've had any man she wanted." He turned and battled the urge to wrap his hands around Nick's throat and squeeze. But that would make him no better than the very man he despised. "Respectable men, who earned an honest living."

"But she chose *me*," Nick said proudly. "That should tell you something."

James snorted in derision. "Only that she had bad taste in men."

"I was always nagging her to marry me, and let me make an honest woman of her. But she wouldn't. She said that if you kept her name instead of mine, you'd be safe from those who bore a grudge against me."

And with good reason. As James stood in this elegant civilized room that smelled of beeswax polish, hothouse roses, and tangy wood smoke from the fire, he remembered the night when he was only twelve, and one of Nick's rivals had sent one of his best men to assassinate Nick Flynn and his family as they were leaving for the theater.

As long as he lived, he'd never forget the loud staccato crack-crack-crack of gunfire mingling with his mother's shrill, terrified screams as she flung him to the floor and shielded him with her own quaking body.

The Flynns and Nick's bodyguard had miraculously survived that day. The man who tried to kill them hadn't.

Even thirteen years later, James still remembered the sickening taste of fear in his mouth and the sharp, acrid stink of gunpowder stinging his nostrils. His first sight of a dead man, his bullet-riddled body lying so still in a pool of blood that slowly spread across white marble tiles.

He shuddered.

"A man wants his only son to have his name," Nick continued. "It's a matter of pride. But I loved my Lucy, so I didn't press her to marry me." A ghost of a smile played about his mouth. "She also said that if I ever broke my promise to keep you out of my business affairs, it'd be easier for her to leave me if we weren't married."

"Smart woman," James muttered.

Suddenly the walls closed in on him. He felt too hot. He couldn't breathe.

"I have to go," he said, striding across the room. When he reached the doors, he hesitated, then turned.

Nick was standing in front of the fireplace again, staring into the dwindling flames. "I can't promise you anything."

"You never could."

James opened the doors and left.

He didn't return to the boardinghouse. He took a walk up windy Lake Shore Drive to calm down and clear his head.

Why couldn't his father stay out of his life?

While Lucille Bradshaw had hated the criminal underworld that Nick Flynn ruled, she loved the man; James could never separate the two.

Nick Flynn made his living illegally, by hurting people and profiting from their weaknesses and misery.

At least his mother had succeeded in isolating her son from Nick's violent world. She gave up the stage and lived a quiet, anonymous existence. To the outside world, her son was not Nick Flynn's child, but the result of a previous liaison with an unnamed actor. Years later, when James grew old enough, he spent more time in European boarding schools and summering on a friend's Yorkshire farm than he did at home in Chicago.

All to keep him safe.

He stopped beneath a streetlight and looked out over the dark waters. His mother had done her job well. No one James knew had a clue about his notorious father.

James could just imagine the hell that Rockwell Shays would make of his life if he ever learned the truth.

"Bradshaw? Is that you?"

James froze, then turned to see a man walking toward him. When the man, bundled up against the cold, stepped into the light, James recognized Dr. Hogg.

His heart leaped to his throat. What if Dr. Hogg had seen him leaving Nick Flynn's mansion? What would the professor think? Maybe James had time to pretend he didn't know him and to hurry off.

Too late. Dr. Hogg had already reached his side. "I thought I recognized you."

"Why, Dr. Hogg . . ." James said. "I didn't know you lived around here."

"This neighborhood, on a professor's salary? Come, come, Mr. Bradshaw. Surely you jest."

James shrugged. "You could have a rich uncle for all I know."

"The truth is much more mundane," he replied. "I spent Thanksgiving with my daughter and her family, and I'm on my way home after an exhausting afternoon playing with my little grandson." He looked back over his shoulder at a brightly lit house. "She married a stockbroker and they live right over there."

So Dr. Hogg hadn't seen James come out of Nick Flynn's house. He let out a sigh of relief.

"Are you here visiting relatives as well?" the professor asked.

"No. Just walking off my dinner, seeing how the other half lives."

The professor cast an admiring glance at a mansion across the drive. "And they live very well indeed, don't they? Though my daughter tells me that more than a few of her neighbors"—he glanced at Nick's fortress—"earn their livings through dishonest means."

"So I've heard."

Dr. Hogg put up his collar. "How is Miss Cooper? Emerson told me what had happened to her in the clinic." He shook his head. "That Shays boy should be expelled."

"I couldn't agree with you more. But at least Miss Cooper is better, and she intends to be in class tomorrow."

"What an amazing woman. Much more exciting than the women of my generation. That is to say, more *intellectually* exciting, of course. Why, if I were twenty

years younger . . .'' Dr. Hogg caught himself. Even in
the cold, by lamplight, his cheeks turned redder. He
cleared his throat. "Well, it's a little too brisk to stay
out here and chat, Bradshaw. I've got my daughter's
carriage, so if you'd like me to drop you off somewhere . . .''

James politely declined, and watched the professor get
into the carriage and drive away.

His secret was safe.

For now.

As he walked away, he glanced back at Nick's house,
and felt his anger returning.

Abby finished her letter to her mother and set down her
pen. She wondered what her parents would think when
they read that their daughter wanted to bring a strange
man home for Christmas.

She'd explained that her classmate and fellow boarder
James Bradshaw had no family, and nowhere else to go.
She'd also emphasized that she had no romantic feelings
whatsoever for him. He'd done her several kindnesses,
and she'd like to repay him by extending her family's
hospitality.

Asking her parents' permission was a mere formality.
Their hearts were as big as the Missouri sky. They'd
welcome any friend of Abby's into their home.

She had her misgivings. Such a well-meaning gesture
was open to misinterpretation. She could just hear the
quilting-circle ladies gnawing on this juicy tidbit. If
Abby Cooper was planning to marry Kyle Lambert,
they'd say, why was she bringing a strange young man
home for Christmas?

Because she couldn't bear the thought of James Bradshaw spending Christmas alone in the boardinghouse

with only Ulysses for company, taking his meals in restaurants.

She'd write to Kyle and explain. She knew he'd understand. After all, if he could buy Mary Dobbs's box lunch because he felt sorry for her, Abby could perform a similar act of kindness by bringing James Bradshaw home for Christmas.

Abby folded the letter and was just about to slip it into an envelope when she hesitated. She hadn't even asked James if he wanted to spend Christmas with her family. She'd presumed that he would. Perhaps he wouldn't.

She set the letter aside, and limped downstairs.

8

ABBY STOOD IN THE PARLOR DOORWAY AND watched James stomp through the foyer like a bull looking for a matador. He'd slammed the front door shut. He muttered under his breath as he tore off his coat and flung it at the rack. When it missed and slid to the floor, he swore a blue streak that would have put Abby's grandfather Jace to shame.

"James, what's wrong?"

He stopped and turned, breathing hard, his nostrils flaring. Even in the foyer's dim light, his dark eyes blazed. The shadows and his own anger twisted his handsome features into a menacing scowl.

"Sorry," he said, unwrapping his scarf and draping it over his coat. "I didn't see you when I came in."

Abby watched his features relax as he fought for self-control. "Did something happen while you were out?"

"I had a close call with a speeding automobile, that's all," he replied.

Why didn't she believe him?

His hard, angry mouth softened into a smile. "Walking without the cane, I see. Your leg must be feeling better."

"It still hurts, but not as much if I move slowly."

He looked around. "Where's Josie?"

"She went to visit Mrs. Gray. She said she'd be back around nine."

James glanced at his watch. "And I'd better get some studying done before class tomorrow. If you'll excuse me . . ." He headed for the stairs.

"James, wait."

He stopped, his brows raised in polite inquiry.

"I'd like to discuss something with you," Abby said. She turned and walked into the parlor.

He followed. "What would you like to discuss?"

When she stopped and turned, James was standing less than an arm's length away. Fresh qualms caused butterflies to flutter in Abby's stomach. She knotted her fingers together and breathed deeply. Even though his closeness made her nervous, she didn't step back. "I realize we haven't exactly been friends."

Amusement danced in the depths of his eyes. "You could say that."

"I'll admit that I thought you were like many of the other men in my class, eager to see me fail."

"What made you change your mind?" he asked softly, his gaze holding hers.

"Ever since you moved in here, I've gotten to know you better. I've seen firsthand that you're not like the others. You've defended me against Shays's attacks."

"Not always." His gaze slid away. "I should've done something sooner, but I was more concerned with my own studies than fighting someone else's battles." He looked up. "I do apologize."

"I've never asked anyone to fight my battles," she said, "but I've never come up against someone as mean and determined as Shays."

"He is a bad one."

"So, to repay you for your many kindnesses, I would like to invite you to spend Christmas with me and my family."

The amused glint faded from his eyes. His smile died. His expression turned guarded.

"You obviously have nowhere else to go for Christmas," Abby continued, "and with the boardinghouse empty, I thought you might enjoy being with a house full of people instead of sitting here with Ulysses. And eating wonderful home-cooked meals instead of in restaurants."

She heard herself rattle on as if her tongue were on wheels, but she couldn't stop. He just kept staring at her. "I think you'd really enjoy visiting. Both my parents and grandfather run horse farms, so there are plenty of animals for us to practice on. And there are my sisters, Regina and Lizzie. They may have their quirks, but they're warm and friendly. And I know they'd enjoy meeting you. That is, if you—"

"I'd like to spend Christmas in Little Falls."

Abby blinked. "You would?"

He nodded. "But wouldn't your fiancé object to your bringing a strange man home for the holidays?"

"Kyle doesn't have an envious bone in his body. Once I explain that you're one of my classmates and that there's nothing between us, he'll understand."

"If you're sure. I wouldn't want to cause trouble between you."

Abby smiled. "Kyle and I love each other. Our bond is strong enough to withstand an innocent visit from one of my classmates."

"Then I accept your kind invitation."

Before Abby could divine his intention, James took

her clasped hands in his and drew them to his lips. The warmth brushed her fingers with feather lightness, sending an unexpected shiver up her arms. She stared speechlessly while he gently pulled her knotted fingers apart, and returned her hands to her sides.

He smiled. Then he turned and left the parlor.

Abby stood there dazed like one in a trance, staring at James's tall, retreating form. No man had ever kissed her hand before. She could still feel the touch of his lips against her skin.

A kiss on the hand meant nothing, of course. Some courtly gesture James had learned in England, to thank her for her invitation. She mustn't misinterpret his intentions.

She mentally shook herself. She'd write Kyle a note right away and mail it at the same time as her mother's letter. That way, they'd both learn that Abby was bringing a guest home for Christmas.

She wanted no misunderstandings.

Back in his room, James sat at his desk and opened his veterinary surgery textbook. He tried to study, but couldn't concentrate. The words all ran together in a black blur. He closed the book, leaned back in his chair, and laced his fingers behind his head.

Abby Ice Maiden Cooper had just invited him to spend Christmas with her family.

He wondered why.

"She must feel sorry for you, Bradshaw," he said to himself.

The thought of him spending Christmas alone in an empty house feeding her cat must have touched a soft spot in her feminine heart. Or perhaps she just wanted to repay him for helping her after she'd been injured in the clinic.

Funny, he hadn't thought of Abigail Cooper as having a soft heart. When it came to her studies, her intellect ruled.

He wondered why he was suddenly beset by second thoughts. He didn't feel uncomfortable being the odd man out. He'd been that most of his life because of Nick. He wasn't worried what Abby's fiancé would think of her bringing home a classmate. He wasn't nervous about meeting Abby's parents, or her two sisters, quirks and all.

So why did he feel like going downstairs and telling Abby that he'd changed his mind?

He rose, jammed his hands into his pockets, and went over to the window, where he stared out into the night. Could he stand being in the bosom of a large, loving family of decent, law-abiding people? In a small Missouri town where breaking a store window was their biggest crime? Where the crack of gunfire meant that a hunter had shot a pheasant?

He decided he wanted to find out.

The following Monday, as Abby and James walked slowly to class, he questioned her about her family, so she described her Grandmama Maddy, who'd moved back to Little Falls from New York City after her husband's death from a heart attack; her parents, especially her unconventional mother, who'd once been the town's unofficial vet and usually wore dungarees; and her sister Regina, married to the local banker and the mother of a little girl named Katie. By the time they walked into the building, she had just finished telling him about her youngest sister, Lizzie, the art student.

"You'll like her," Abby said as they joined the other students filling the hall. "She's fun and, unlike Regina, doesn't put on airs."

"She sounds like someone I'd like to know," Bradshaw said. He studied her. "What's the matter? You look like you've seen a ghost."

Abby saw Evans and Hendries, Shays's two cronies, up ahead and suddenly her lighthearted mood vanished. "I'm just wondering what torments Shays has devised. He's had a long weekend to plot and scheme."

Bradshaw's jaw tensed. "After what he did to you in the clinic, he'd better not try anything."

They entered the classroom together, and Abby went to her usual seat in the last row. She noticed that Shays's two cronies were at the front of the room, holding court with the rest of the students.

Several of the men darted curious looks her way.

"I wonder what's going on?" Abby whispered to James. "I don't see Shays anywhere."

"That is odd." He frowned. "I don't remember him ever missing a day of school." He set his books down on the desk next to hers. "Let me see if I can find out."

As James headed toward the other men, Abby noticed they eyed him suspiciously before they exchanged warning looks and fell silent.

"What's going on?" he asked.

Evans stepped forward. "Something you'll be pleased to hear, Bradshaw." He glared down the long row of desks at Abby. "You and Miss Cooper."

Hendries joined him. "Somebody beat up Shays last night."

James gaped at him. "Shays? Beaten?"

"You heard me." Evans sneered. "He's lucky to be alive."

Abby suddenly felt weak as the blood drained from her face. Someone had beaten up Rockwell Shays?

"Yeah," Hendries said. "At first we thought you did it, Bradshaw."

A dark flush of anger flooded James's cheeks, and his hands balled into fists. Quick as a pouncing cat, he lunged at Hendries, but two men grabbed his arms just in time and restrained him.

Hendries stayed just out of reach and gloated. "See that? The son of a bitch went for me. You're all witnesses."

Abby rose and marched between the desks. "Mr. Hendries, who gave you the right to make such a horrid and unfounded accusation! Mr. Bradshaw would no more beat a man than I would. And in any case, he was at the boardinghouse all evening, studying."

When Abby had gone to the bathroom to wash before bed, she saw the sliver of light under James's door.

"You two could've been in cahoots," Evans said. "I wouldn't put anything past either of you."

"You're a lucky man, Bradshaw," Hendries added. "Shays said you weren't the thug who attacked him."

James finally relaxed. "Good thing, because he would've been lying." He shrugged off the men holding him. "Did he say what the man looked like?"

"All he could tell was that it wasn't you."

"Was Shays badly hurt?" Abby asked.

"Sorry to disappoint you, Miss Cooper," Evans said. "He's got two black eyes, a swollen jaw, and a couple of broken ribs, but he'll live."

"Despite what you may think, Mr. Evans," Abby said coldly, "I have no desire to see Mr. Shays come to any harm. Even for making my life hell. Too bad he can't say the same."

She turned on her heel and returned to her seat.

"When did it happen?" James asked. "And where?"

"Go to hell," Evans muttered, and took his seat, where he glared back over his shoulder at Abby as if she'd been personally responsible for Shays's beating.

But Hendries obviously wanted to give James the details. "He'd just finished having dinner with us, and he left to go home. He was walking to the streetcar when this man pulled him into an alley and beat him."

"Maybe robbery was the motive for the attack," James suggested.

Hendries shook his head. "The man didn't take Shays's wallet or his watch. When Shays came to, he managed to stagger back to our place. We took him to the hospital, then called the police."

"Shays and I have had our differences," James said, finally calm and controlled, "but I'm sorry this happened to him, and I hope he recovers soon."

Then the professor entered, signaling that class was about to begin, so James returned to his seat.

Abby found it difficult to concentrate during the lecture, for she couldn't stop thinking about Shays. Though she disliked the man, he didn't deserve this.

Glancing over at James, she noticed him staring out into space, his eyes glazed as though he were a million miles away. Every once in a while, he frowned with a brooding intensity and made little drawings in his notebook. When the professor called on him, he didn't know the answer to the question. And he didn't seem to care.

Abby thought such behavior odd for a man competing to be valedictorian.

Why was he so preoccupied with what had happened to Shays? Abby intended to find out.

•　•　•

She decided to wait until classes were over and she and James returned to the boardinghouse before she discussed Shays. Even walking home, she noticed that James's attention was focused inward rather than on their surroundings.

"Don't take it to heart," Abby said when they passed the apartment building next door.

At the sound of her voice, James returned to the present. He looked at her, his eyes now clear and focused. "Don't take what to heart?"

"Hendries's accusation that you beat up Shays. He only said that to needle you."

James smiled wryly. "If that was his intention, he succeeded." His smile darkened to a scowl. "I wanted to wipe that sneer right off his face."

Growing up on a horse farm, where men worked hard and looked for excuses to let off steam, Abby had seen her share of volatile masculine tempers and bloody fistfights. To watch James almost lose control in class surprised her. He seemed like such a calm, even-tempered man.

She also knew that any man could be pushed to the breaking point with sufficient provocation. And Hendries had almost succeeded.

"Hitting him wouldn't have accomplished anything," she said. "If anything, fighting in class might've gotten you expelled."

James let out a long, relieved breath. "Damn! I didn't even think of that."

"It would've been a shame to be thrown out with just one semester to go until graduation."

"I'll certainly think twice before I let someone like Hendries push me into doing something so stupid."

When Abby and James entered the boardinghouse,

they found a worried-looking Josie pacing the foyer and wringing her hands.

Before they could even greet her, she grabbed their arms and whispered, "There's a policeman named O'Reilly here to see you. Both of you. But he wouldn't tell me why. He's been sitting in my parlor for the better part of an hour. I told him I didn't know when you'd be home, but he insisted on waiting."

Abby exchanged uneasy looks with James.

"It must be about Shays," he said, helping her with her coat.

"But we don't know anything about what happened last night," Abby said.

James glanced toward the parlor door. "He must think we do."

Josie's head darted from Abby to James and back to Abby. "What about Shays?"

"We'll tell you later," Abby said. She looked at James. "Shall we?"

Josie led the way into the parlor. "Sergeant O'Reilly, Miss Cooper and Mr. Bradshaw are home."

The policeman, who'd been munching a plate of Josie's oatmeal cookies and sipping tea, rose from the sofa and pulled at the hem of his blue jacket. A stocky man not as tall as James, Sergeant O'Reilly had a florid, suspicious face, and hard, merciless gaze that demanded the truth.

He stepped forward and nodded at Abby. "Miss Abigail Cooper and James Bradshaw. I'm Sergeant O'Reilly of the Chicago Police Department, and I'm here to question you both about yesterday's attack on Rockwell Shays."

Josie gasped and turned so white Abby feared their

landlady might faint. "Someone attacked Shays? But you and James had nothing—"

"Don't worry." Abby placed a reassuring hand on the older woman's arm. "It'll be all right. Why don't you go make us some tea?"

Josie nodded. "Tea. Yes. I'll go to the kitchen and make tea."

With Josie out of the room, James said to Sergeant O'Reilly, "Miss Cooper and I know nothing about the attack. The first we heard about it was this morning, when we went to class."

Abby added, "We were both here at the boarding-house last night, studying."

The policeman raised an impatient hand. "I'm not accusing either of you of anything. I'm here to ask you some questions, so if you'll take a seat, we'll begin."

When everyone was seated, Sergeant O'Reilly said, "Tell me what you heard about Shays's beating."

James told him the Evans and Hendries version. Then he added, "Sergeant, am I a suspect? It's common knowledge that Shays and I dislike each other."

"We know all about that," O'Reilly said, "but Mr. Shays himself denied that you were the man who attacked him."

Abby slowly let out the breath she'd been holding.

"Then why are you questioning us?" James demanded. "We had nothing to do with it."

The sergeant looked up from his notebook straight at Abby. "Then why did the assailant say, 'Leave Abigail Cooper alone,' just before kicking Shays into unconsciousness?"

Abby felt a jolt of shock. She couldn't think. She couldn't move. She just sat there, stunned with disbelief.

"Well, Miss Cooper?" the policeman barked.

James rose. "This is preposterous."

Sergeant O'Reilly made a notation in his book. "The assailant's statement—"

"The assailant's statement?" James said. "How do you know the assailant said anything? You have only Shays's word, and considering how he feels about Miss Cooper, I'll bet he's lying."

The policeman glowered. "The assailant's statement to Mr. Shays would indicate to me that he was acting on Miss Cooper's behalf. Or at least delivering a painful warning from someone." He turned that merciless gaze on James. "You, perhaps?"

James's lip curled in disdain. "If I wanted to deliver a painful warning to Shays, Sergeant, I wouldn't pay someone else to do my dirty work. I'd do it myself."

Abby rose, her shock turning to outrage. "You think that *I* paid someone to beat up Rockwell Shays?"

"The assailant knew your name, Miss Cooper," O'Reilly said, "and he obviously wanted Shays to stop harassing you."

James's eyes narrowed. "Do you have any proof to connect either of us to Shays's beating, Sergeant?"

The policeman closed his notebook and rose. "No," he admitted, his remorseless stare focused on Abby as if he could intimidate her into confessing. "Not until we catch whoever did this."

"Then we don't have to answer any more of your questions," James said.

"For now," the sergeant retorted, putting on his hat and heading for the door.

He almost ran into Josie carrying the tea tray. "Aren't you staying for tea, Sergeant?"

"No," James said, placing a hand on Abby's shoulder. "The sergeant was just leaving."

Later that evening, after both James and Josie went out, Abby went into the quiet, empty parlor and sat down in her favorite chair. A minute later, Ulysses trotted into the parlor, jumped into Abby's lap, and curled himself into a contented ball.

Hours after Sergeant O'Reilly had left, Abby still remained rattled and on edge. She couldn't stop shaking. She tried petting her cat, hoping the stroking motion would calm her, but her nervousness only upset Ulysses. He regarded her with supreme feline disgust before jumping down and trotting off to patrol for mice.

Abby couldn't believe that the police suspected her of being involved in Shays's beating.

"Leave Abigail Cooper alone," the assailant had said. According to Shays. As James had pointed out, he could be lying. But what if he wasn't?

She sighed and rubbed her forehead as if she could coax out an answer. None of her classmates cared whether Shays harassed her.

Only James.

9

LITTLE FALLS, MISSOURI

MADELINE SULLIVAN WILLS HAD BEEN WAITING for ghosts to appear ever since she returned to Little Falls. A year had passed, but none had come calling.

She stood at the parlor window of the old boarding-house that had been her home and her sanctuary half a lifetime ago, and stared through the curtains at the brick walk now hidden beneath a thin layer of snow. She tried to imagine herself as a young woman of twenty-four again. At sixty-nine, it was becoming increasingly difficult, but she was a tough old bird who refused to let the passage of time fade her cherished memories as it had faded her fiery red hair with threads of gray.

She next pictured her husband, Paul, as she'd first known him, a handsome young doctor of twenty-eight, opening the front gate that had always squeaked, and walking toward the boardinghouse. In the springtime of her memory, his hair was still jet-black, his blue eyes shone behind round steel-rimmed spectacles, his demeanor remained serious and thoughtful as he studied the veterinary journal he always carried.

She reached up to smooth the unruly mane of cork-screw curls that she'd always worn tied back with a ribbon as a girl, then remembered she hadn't worn it that way for over forty years. Paul wouldn't have forgotten.

Maddy smiled. A ghost at last. She blinked, and Paul vanished. Not a ghost after all, just another sweet memory.

She walked over to the upright piano standing against the far wall and lifted the keyboard cover in silent invitation. She looked around the parlor. "Play 'Beautiful Dreamer' for me. Please?"

She stepped back and listened very carefully, for her hearing wasn't as sharp as her eyesight. She hoped to hear her old friend Mrs. Sims pounding the sweet strains of Maddy's favorite song out of those stiff, yellowed ivory keys. But the only music she heard was the faint whistle of the winter wind.

"My dear, sweet Augusta . . ." She closed the keyboard cover and sighed wistfully. "Even you won't visit."

A loud knock on the door startled her. She hadn't expected a ghost to knock.

She opened the door to find her middle granddaughter, Regina, standing there, all decked out as elegantly as an Astor or a Vanderbilt in her black fox-trimmed coat and matching muff. "Hello, Grandmama."

Maddy hid her disappointment behind a bright smile. "Come in, come in, before you catch your death."

Regina Cooper Godwin stepped into the parlor and brushed a dutiful kiss on Maddy's cheek. Then she handed her the huge muff, which Maddy set atop the piano.

Sometimes, when Maddy looked at Regina, she clearly saw the spitting image of her own daughter Catherine, Regina's mother. Both shared the same tall, slender physique, jet black hair, and blue eyes. Yet when Regina smiled, Maddy swore she saw her own Paul, Regina's grandfather, smiling back at her.

Unfortunately, Regina resembled neither her mother nor her grandfather in temperament. Maddy blamed Regina's haughtiness and snobbishness solely on her paternal grandmother, Clementine, who'd been both haughty and a snob in her youth.

"You didn't bring Katie," Maddy said. She loved visiting with her little great-granddaughter, who had just turned two last month.

"Oh, it's much too cold for my baby to be out," Regina replied with just a hint of reproof in her voice. She unpinned her floppy black velvet beret, then took off her coat. She carefully folded the garment inside out and draped it over the back of the sofa rather than hang it on the coat tree. "I wouldn't want her to get sick."

Maddy's temper flared, and she had to bite her tongue before she said something that would offend Regina and send her off in a huff. Old age may have lined Maddy's face and slowed her down, but it hadn't dulled the flame of her hot Irish temper.

She smiled instead. "And how are you feeling? Do you still suffer from morning sickness?"

Regina rested a proprietary hand on the gentle swell of her abdomen. She was five months pregnant, and proud of the fact that she barely showed. "Yes, but once it's over, I feel fine for the rest of the day."

Maddy, who, as a young girl, had learned the art of herbal healing from her own grandmother, refrained from recommending any remedies. She knew the modern-thinking Regina disdained old-fashioned medicines made from leaves, roots, and barks, preferring to put her faith in newfangled chemical pills and powders.

"Come into the kitchen," Maddy said, "and I'll make us tea."

Regina hesitated. "Why don't we drink it here? The parlor is much more comfortable, especially for a woman in my delicate condition."

Maddy's temper simmered. The only reason Regina didn't want to have tea at the kitchen table was because she felt it was beneath her.

"I would never want you to be uncomfortable," Maddy said, "especially in your condition. But I will need you to get the teapot for me. At my age, I can't go standing on stools and rummaging in cupboards."

Resentment smoldered in Regina's blue eyes. "I'll be happy to get your teapot for you, Grandmama."

"Speak up. I don't hear as well as I used to."

Regina repeated her offer more loudly.

Maddy led the way to the kitchen. "I remember the day Miz' Sims reached for the teapot, fell off the stool, and broke her leg. Your grandfather, who was the only real doctor in town, came to set it, but he was so gruff and disrespectful to her that I—"

"Lost your temper and gave him a tongue-lashing he never forgot," Regina said wearily, by rote. "I know, Grandmama."

"Oh, have I told you that story before?" Maddy asked innocently, when she damn well knew she had. She could play the dotty old lady to the hilt when she chose.

When they walked in the kitchen, Maddy opened a cupboard door and pointed to the teapot high on a shelf.

By standing on tiptoes and, extending her arm, Regina was able to reach it.

Maddy thanked her, and shooed her back to the parlor, calling her back into the kitchen when the tea was ready. "If you'll be so good as to carry the tray for me . . ."

Once they were seated and the tea poured and served, Maddy knew from past experience that if she wanted any information from Regina about her sisters, she would first have to question her about her own family.

"Clyde is doing well?" Maddy asked, referring to Regina's ambitious young husband, who managed the only bank in Little Falls. "Remember to speak up."

Regina sipped her tea and beamed. "He is doing very well. In fact, he just received a handsome bonus from the board of directors for his outstanding work."

"I'll have to remember to offer him my congratulations," Maddy said.

Considering the fact that Regina's great-grandfather started that bank, and the surviving Cooper elders still had a controlling interest in it through marriage, Clyde's future looked assured.

"Of course he doesn't intend to stay in Little Falls forever," Regina said. "Eventually he'd like to manage the Boswell Bank headquarters in St. Louis."

Maddy raised her brows. "You'd leave Little Falls? But this is your home."

Regina pursed her lips and looked down her pert nose. "I'm quickly growing tired of provincial, small-town life, Grandmama. I'd like to live in a big, exciting city like St. Louis, where everybody doesn't know everybody else's business."

"If you feel that way, why on earth did you ever join the quilting circle?"

The women of this group met twice a week in each

other's homes to sew quilts to sell for charity, but mostly to gossip. The membership fluctuated, but the circle had existed before the Civil War and would no doubt roll on for another hundred years.

"Why, for a social outlet, of course," Regina replied.

"I see."

"And you're one to talk about my staying in Little Falls, Grandmama. You yourself left to go to New York."

"Yes, I did, because my husband's work took him there. And after a few years, even I, a simple country girl, grew to love the crowds and the noise." She looked around the parlor and smiled. "But I always yearned to come home to Little Falls."

Regina looked around the parlor and frowned. "I'm surprised you moved back into this old place. You're not poor by any means, Grandmama. You could afford a nice new house at the other end of Main Street, near mine."

This is my home, Maddy thought. *This is where the ghosts know to find me.*

"Oh, I'm too old to rattle around in some fancy new house," she said. "This place suits me just fine."

"I don't know how you stand the shabbiness." Regina sniffed disdainfully. "That old piano is out of tune, and this sofa has been around since the Civil War."

"As have I," Maddy reminded her, feeling her temper simmer dangerously.

Regina turned pale. "Oh, Grandmama, I didn't mean—"

"That's quite all right. I know exactly what you meant. Now, when will Lizzie and Abby be arriving?"

Regina told her that she didn't know. Then she said,

"Do you think Abby really intends to marry Kyle Lambert?"

Maddy saw red as she always did when Lambert's name was mentioned. "Of course she intends to marry him. The women in this family do exactly as they please. Abby is no different. Unless," she added, "we can talk her out of it."

Regina shook her head. "My sister, marrying a man who runs a *saloon*. Abby may be headstrong, but she's got many other qualities that would appeal to a man. There must be hundreds of eligible young men with bright futures ahead of them in Chicago. I just can't understand why she'd settle for a man like Kyle Lambert."

"The only possible explanation is that she really does love him," Maddy said.

Regina rolled her eyes. "A woman can just as easily love a man with a promising future."

She set down her teacup and rose, reaching for her coat. "Well, as much as I enjoy visiting with you, I have to return home. I like to be there when Katie wakes up from her nap."

Maddy rose, ignoring the slight stiffness that affected her left calf when she sat too long. Once Regina bundled herself up, Maddy showed her to the door and handed her the muff. "Give that little angel a big hug and a kiss for me."

Regina touched her lips to Maddy's cheek. "I certainly will." Then she said good-bye, and left.

Maddy took the tray back into the kitchen. As she washed out the teapot, she stared out the window at the backyard. Her herb garden had long gone to seed, and the shed where she'd prepared her medicinal infusions and tinctures had been torn down. Standing in its place was a new barn.

But Maddy couldn't concern herself with the past. Her precious Abby's future was a stake.

Catherine "Cat" Cooper sat at her kitchen table and read her daughter Abby's letter for the third time.

The familiar sound of her husband's quick footsteps on the back stairs didn't break her concentration. When Michael opened the kitchen door and walked in from the cold, stomping his feet on the mat to shake the snow off his boots, Cat couldn't concentrate on anything else.

Even after twenty-three years of marriage and the trials and tribulations of raising three headstrong daughters, Cat's love hadn't diminished for the man who'd been her childhood friend, her lover, and her husband. Even at forty-five, Michael was a fine figure of a man, all lean muscle, his dark brown hair as thick and unruly as a boy's, though lightly peppered with gray, like an old dog's muzzle. Time had scored deep lines at the corners of his eyes and down his lean, weathered cheeks, but to Cat, they made him look less boyish and more mature, like a fine aged wine.

Michael hung up his hat and had almost unbuttoned his jacket when he caught Cat staring at him. He stared back. Then he grinned. "You keep looking at me like I'm dinner, Willie, and you know what's going to happen."

"Michael Cooper! It's broad daylight."

"You know as well as I do that's the best time. A man likes to see what he's doing."

Cat rose from the table and sauntered over to him, smiling and swaying her rounded hips as provocatively as a saloon girl. When she reached him, she locked her arms around his neck and pulled his mouth down to hers.

His lips felt smooth and heavy, and tasted so sweet, Cat could have dined on them forever. Especially with Michael's expressive hands cupping her bottom and pressing her against him. But she had to stop.

She released him reluctantly and stepped away.

Michael looked justifiably annoyed. "Don't tease. Not when I've had such a hard morning."

"It's about to get harder." When Michael grinned and reached for her again, Cat grabbed the letter off the kitchen table and handed it to him. "This just came from Abby."

Michael sobered and took the letter. "Trouble?"

"Could be."

The kitchen fell silent, save for the soft rustle of paper as Michael read.

When he finished, he looked at Cat. "Our daughter wants to bring a *stranger* home for Christmas?"

"He's no stranger to Abby," Cat pointed out. "He's one of her classmates, and he's been living at Josie's boardinghouse."

Michael scowled at the letter like a typically worried father. "I don't remember her ever mentioning a James Bradshaw before. Do you?"

"When she was home this summer, I seem to recall her saying something about him being second in line for valedictorian."

"So he's her chief rival."

"You could say that."

"Then why in Sam Hill is she inviting him here for Christmas?"

"Michael," Cat said with studied wifely patience, placing a calming hand on his arm, "she says why on the bottom of the first page."

"Oh." He reread that part, then nodded sagely. "I might've known. He has nowhere else to go, and Abby feels sorry for him."

Cat shook her head. "That's our daughter, champion of the underdog."

For all Abby's strength and singlemindedness, she had a soft spot in her heart for the downtrodden, the neglected, the helpless. Cat remembered when one of the dogs had a litter of puppies, Abby always made sure that the runt got his share of his mother's milk. If a foal lost its mother, Abby stayed with it day and night, sleeping in its stall and bottle feeding the newborn until the foal could survive on its own.

Now she was adding this Bradshaw fellow to the list.

Michael finally got his jacket off, then sat down at the table. Sensing he wanted to discuss this development further, Cat sat down next to him.

Michael rubbed his jaw. "If she's planning to marry Kyle, why's she bringing a strange man home with her? If the woman I was planning to marry came home with a strange man, I'd wonder about her intentions."

"It could be purely innocent," Cat said. "This classmate of hers has nowhere else to go, and Abby invited him because she feels sorry for him.

"Or maybe Abby has fallen in love with this young man, and plans to break it off with Kyle."

Michael gave her a skeptical look. "You don't really believe that, do you?"

Cat sighed. "No."

Michael rose, his eyes twinkling. "Why don't we forget about Abby and Lambert for a little while?"

Cat smiled seductively. "And how exactly do you plan to do that?"

"Come upstairs and I'll show you."

• • •

Later, when Michael finally rolled over with an exhausted groan and closed his eyes, Cat rose from their bed, slipped on her robe, and walked over to the window.

Why couldn't she bring herself to like Kyle Lambert?

Because he reminded her of Drake Kendall, a man from Cat's past who'd tried to woo her away from Michael.

Physically, both men were blond, blue-eyed giants standing almost six and a half feet tall. Where Drake demonstrated polish and refinement as befitted his privileged Boston background, Kyle was loud and boisterous, qualities both Cat and Michael found grating. She also saw shades of Drake's opportunism beneath Kyle's bluff, easygoing facade.

Cat ran her fingers through her short, dark mop. She didn't turn around when she heard Michael get out of bed and pad barefoot across the floor.

He slid his arms around her waist and drew her against him for a perfect fit. "Tell me what you're thinking."

"I've finally figured out why I have such reservations about Kyle," she replied.

Michael nuzzled her shoulder. "He reminds you of Drake."

Surprised, Cat turned in his arms. "How did you know?"

Her husband's eyes turned cold. "Because he reminds *me* of Drake. That and the fact that he runs a saloon."

"We shouldn't hold his ambition against him," Cat said. "He's only twenty-two, and he's turned One-Eyed Jack's into a thriving business. You can't even get into the place on a Saturday night."

"It's not the gambling and drinking I object to," Michael said, "it's the *girls*."

Cat stepped out of his arms and looked at him with reproof. "You're one to talk about saloon girls, Michael Cooper. Are you so quick to forget that before we were married you used to enjoy going upstairs with Ruby?"

"That's different. I was a young man with wild oats to sow. We're discussing our *daughter*. And I don't like the idea of Abby being married to a man who profits from women selling themselves."

"Abby told us that since Kyle only runs the saloon, he can't do anything about the girls. It's the owner who wants them there. But Kyle's promised her that he'll get rid of them someday when he owns Jack's."

"I know that's what Lambert told her."

"Why don't you believe him?"

Michael shook his head. "Damned if I know. Just a feeling I have deep in my gut." He placed his hands on her shoulders. "In the meantime, how do we know that Lambert doesn't trot himself upstairs every so often to sample the goods?"

"Why, Michael Cooper, aren't you the suspicious one."

His hands fell away. "Just realistic."

"If Kyle is carrying on with his girls, I'm sure we would've heard by now."

"I hope you're right. For Abby's sake."

"We'll just have to trust him and give him the benefit of the doubt."

Until Kyle proved otherwise.

In his tiny office in the back room at One-Eyed Jack's, Kyle Lambert didn't bother reading Abby's letter a second time before crumpling it into a ball.

The woman he planned to marry was bringing a class-mate home for Christmas.

A *male* classmate.

Kyle leaned back in his swivel chair and steepled his fingers. A rival? No, he was as certain of Abby's love and devotion as he was of old Heck Hechinger's weekly Friday night upstairs appointment with Holly.

Still, a man couldn't take a woman—or a sure thing— for granted.

He opened his desk drawer and rummaged around until he found the envelope. When he opened it, the small diamond ring sparkled. He smiled, pleased with himself. No need to tell Abby he'd won it in a private poker game. As far as she was concerned, he'd gone all the way to St. Louis last month to pick it out just for her. He'd gone to St. Louis all right, but to avail himself of big-city pleasures, not to buy her a ring.

He'd present this one to her on Christmas Day.

They'd be officially engaged, and her snooty, disapproving family would be helpless to prevent their marriage. And once that happened, they'd want their daughter and future grandchildren to be secure, so they'd see the wisdom of buying him Jack's.

Kyle Lambert, the son of dirt poor farmers, would be set for life.

He leaned back in his swivel chair and smiled.

10

As THE BUGGY ROLLED INTO LITTLE FALLS, JAMES listened. He heard a dog's warning bark, followed by a child's shrill, excited shout. Then silence.

Just vast, blessed silence.

He breathed slowly and deeply. He smelled only cold, sweet fresh air and an intoxicating trace of woodsmoke.

Turning onto the wide unpaved main street James saw one- and two-story storefronts and boardwalks instead of concrete sidewalks that had been swept spotless. The town's only bank, which Abby's brother-in-law managed, looked sturdy enough to keep its customers' savings safe. The Dobbs Mercantile would have fit in one corner of the Marshall Field department store's south rotunda. One-Eyed Jack's, the saloon that Abby's fiancé now operated and where Josie's father had drunk away half his life, boasted a fresh coat of dark blue paint with sparkling white trim, and a sign with bold gold-leaf lettering.

James looked at Abby sitting next to him in the rented buggy. They'd driven for miles without seeing a house, another human being, or even a grazing cow.

He smiled. "Do you remember when you first described Little Falls to me, and I said it sounded like paradise?"

Abby nodded. "You'd just moved in, and we were having supper."

"I was right. This is paradise."

Her pretty face warmed with pleasure. "You don't miss the big-city crowds, the noise, the skyscrapers?" she teased.

"I'll especially miss the rumble and the clatter of the meat wagon pulling into Kachinsky's alley at five in the morning."

"And the shoe factory's six o'clock whistle."

"Not to mention risking my life dodging a speeding automobile or two."

He noticed that the moodiness and tension she'd displayed on the train ride from Chicago had finally left her. He didn't doubt that Shays's beating and the subsequent visit from Sergeant O'Reilly weighed heavily on her mind. Being suspected of committing a crime upset most people. Arriving home had definitely lightened her mood.

James watched as two women came out of the post office and lingered to chat with each other. "What'll be our first stop?"

"If I don't see Kyle, I'll explode," she said. "Then, we'll visit my Grandmama Maddy."

James was looking forward to meeting Abby's intriguing grandmother, but he had reservations about Kyle Lambert. Nick had gotten his start as a saloon keeper, and James tended to tar them all with the same brush.

He urged their horse down Main Street and headed for One-Eyed Jack's. "How'd the saloon get its name?"

"Jack, the original owner, lost one eye and covered it with an eye patch."

"So Kyle works for Jack."

"No. Jack died several years ago, when a brawler used his eye patch for target practice and, unfortunately for poor Jack, didn't miss. Another man named Lindstrom bought the saloon, but Kyle hopes to buy him out eventually."

James pulled the horse and buggy up in front of One-Eyed Jack's and jumped down to help Abby, whose blue eyes sparkled with anticipation.

She straightened her hat with a feminine primping motion and smoothed her coat. "How do I look?"

"Kyle will take one look at you, and he'll never want you to leave Little Falls."

"I can't stay. I still have another semester to go."

Abby opened the saloon's front door and went inside. James followed not far behind.

Loud masculine laughter boomed out as he and Abby stepped into the dimly lit saloon.

"We're closed," that same masculine voice said from the vicinity of the bar. "Come back when we open at five."

James looked around, curious. He had to admit that One-Eyed Jack's could hold its own with the best of Nick Flynn's saloons. The windows looked freshly washed, the floor was scrubbed and polished and the brass rail lining the foot of the long bar gleamed.

Behind the bar stood a giant of a man arranging bottles of whiskey and bourbon, while a woman stacked clean glasses.

Abby cleared her throat. "I think you can make an exception."

Kyle turned around and grinned. "Abby! You're

home!'' He rounded the bar and came at her, welcoming arms extended wide.

James thought the man resembled a grizzly bear towering on its hind legs. Abby had told James that Kyle was tall, but she hadn't prepared him for the man's imposing size. With those broad shoulders, Kyle was one and a half times James's size.

Abby ran to him. He swept her into his arms and swung her around and around so fast her hat toppled to the floor. She laughed and protested that he was making her dizzy. When he finally stopped, he kissed her.

James looked away from the embracing couple, his gaze resting on the pretty brunette behind the bar. She smiled at him. He smiled back.

Kyle finally stopped kissing Abby, but he didn't release her. ''I missed you so much. I thought you'd never get here.''

''And I missed you,'' Abby said, hugging him back.

''Did you have a good trip?''

''Uneventful, and much too long. I thought we'd—'' She stopped and looked over at James. ''Kyle, there's someone I want you to meet.''

He looked at James as if aware of him for the first time. Lambert came striding toward him with a wide grin and his hand extended.

''You must be James Bradshaw.'' He pumped James's hand in a bone-crushing grip and thumped him on the shoulder. ''Abby's told me a lot about you.''

''She's told me a great deal about you, too.''

Lambert's booming laughter reverberated through the saloon. ''Not that much, I hope, or I'm in trouble.''

Abby swatted his arm in mock reproof. ''Oh, Kyle . . .''

He slid an arm around her waist, pulled her to him,

and kissed the top of her head. "Just funning, honey."

Abby looked over at the woman behind the bar and called out greetings. "That's Minnie," she told James. "She works for Kyle."

In what capacity? he wondered. But he nodded at Minnie, and she smiled back.

James looked around. "You've got a nice place here."

"Right kind of you to say so," Lambert replied, still holding on to Abby. "It's not easy keeping it up, what with some of the rowdy, out-of-town riffraff we get, but I do my best, and I'm proud of it."

"You should be."

Lambert looked down at Abby. "Can you and James stay awhile, or are you going straight out to the farm?"

"First I want to see my grandmother, and maybe Regina. And then we'll go out to the farm."

"Don't think you have to spend all your time with me," Lambert said, chucking her beneath the chin. "I know how important your family is to you."

"But you're important to me, too," Abby said. "I don't want you to feel that I'm neglecting you."

"You could never make me feel that way. We'll be spending Christmas Day together, and in another six months, we'll be spending the rest of our lives together."

Abby looked at James. "I couldn't ask for a more understanding man."

James didn't know quite what to say to that, so he thought fast. "He's obviously very much in love."

Lambert grinned and squeezed Abby to his side. "Head over heels with this little lady. But don't forget, honey, we have wedding plans to discuss, so set aside a little time for me."

"I will," Abby promised.

"Well," Lambert said, releasing Abby, "if you two will excuse me, I've got work to do." He extended his hand to James again. "A pleasure meeting you, Bradshaw. Make sure you stop in some night while you're here. The drinks'll be on the house, and"—he glanced at Minnie—"I'll make sure you have a good time."

James knew exactly the kind of good time Lambert was referring to, and he wanted no part of it. But he shook the man's hand and thanked him.

Then Lambert drew Abby into his arms and kissed her good-bye.

James crossed the floor to retrieve Abby's hat.

When they were back in the buggy, heading toward Abby's grandmother's, James said, "Your Kyle seems like a friendly, outgoing sort."

"He is. He has lots of friends, and everyone likes him. He just has a knack for making people comfortable."

"That must be why the saloon is so successful."

"I suspect so."

James hoped Lambert wasn't like Nick, showing a friendly, outgoing exterior to the world, but keeping his dark, innermost nature a secret.

When Abby and James arrived at her grandmother's house they found no one at home, so they proceeded on to the Cooper farm.

James revised his estimation of paradise when he saw Abby's home.

Charming, he thought when the buggy pulled up to the farmhouse, a small, square wood-frame box that had been added to as the family's needs for more room expanded. The wing, while it hadn't been planned with an architect's precise eye to form, gave the structure an original, winsome personality.

Beyond the house stood one large barn and a newly built smaller one a little distance away. James could see several horses standing with their heads hanging over the paddock fences, staring curiously at the new arrivals.

No sooner did James come to a complete stop than the farmhouse's front door opened, and a woman dressed in a blue chambray shirt tucked into dungarees came striding out onto the porch. The minute she saw them she trotted down the steps and hurried toward them, her shivering arms crossed tightly for warmth against the winter winds. James recognized her immediately as Abby's mother.

"Mama," Abby admonished, scrambling down from the buggy before James himself could alight and assist her, "you shouldn't be out here in the cold without a coat. You'll catch your death."

Catherine Cooper smiled and opened her arms wide. "I heard you coming, and didn't want to spare the time, puss."

James climbed down while mother and daughter hugged. When they parted, Mrs. Cooper turned to him and held out her hand, "You must be James."

He almost told her that she looked more like Abby's older sister than her mother. No lie. Though in her early forties, Mrs. Cooper looked ten years younger than that. But something in her direct, assessing gaze warned him she wouldn't buy it, no matter how sincere.

He smiled and extended his hand. "Mrs. Cooper. Thank you for inviting me to spend the holidays with your family."

Her grip was firm, her gaze unwavering as she sized him up. "Abby's friends are always welcome."

Abby looked around. "Where's Papa?"

"Where else?" her mother replied. "Out in the barn."

"Your teeth are going to start chattering any minute," Abby said. "Let's go inside."

Mrs. Cooper winked at James. "She loves to order everyone around."

"I know," he said, grinning as he reached for their bags. "She's awfully bossy."

Abby looked mortally offended. "I am not."

Her mother laughed, a rich, mirthful sound she'd bequeathed to her daughter along with that dark, unself-conscious beauty and elegant grace. "Let's get you two settled."

As they marched to the house, Abby rattled off names James assumed to be family and friends, and her mother updated her on their comings and goings.

Once inside, James barely had time to look around the comfortable parlor with its empty birdcage in one corner before Abby ushered him upstairs and showed him where he'd be staying, a large, bright bedroom with windows overlooking the barns and snow-dusted fields beyond.

After James unpacked, washed, and changed out of his traveling suit, he went back downstairs, where the aroma of freshly brewed coffee lured him into the kitchen.

Mrs. Cooper, assembling coffee cups at the counter, smiled when he walked through the door. "You all settled? I trust the room is to your liking."

"I couldn't ask for a more comfortable one."

"Good." She nodded toward the scarred oak table. "Have a seat." Once James was seated, Mrs. Cooper served him his coffee, then poured one for herself. "So you're studying to be a veterinarian, too."

"Yes. Abby's told me you were one yourself."

Mrs. Cooper smiled ruefully as she sat across from him. "I was the town's only vet for years, but I had no formal schooling. Not like Abby. Everything I knew I learned from my father, who was a doctor, and my mother, an expert at herbal healing."

"Do you still practice?"

She shook her head. "Once I started having children, I found I was too busy to ride around the country doctoring other people's animals. But I've always tended to our family's livestock, so you could say that I've always practiced in some capacity." She smiled. "Who knows? Maybe my daughter will let me help her out once in a while."

"So Little Falls no longer has a veterinarian," James said.

"Oh, no. Dr. Horatio Kendall doctors animals as well as people, but it's not his favorite type of work. He's planning to stop as soon as Abby gets her degree and opens her own veterinary practice." Mrs. Cooper looked troubled. "I know Abby worries about being able to be both a vet and a mother. She saw firsthand that I couldn't do it, and she worries that she won't be able to either."

James sipped the strong black coffee. "She's always given me the impression she can do anything."

Mrs. Cooper smiled. "She's very determined." Her smile faded and she looked unsure of herself. "I realize we've only just met, and I hope you won't think me presumptuous. But I'm Abby's mother, and I worry about her. Since you've been living at Josie's, would you answer a question for me?"

"If I can."

"Does my daughter still have those nightmares, when she wakes up screaming?"

James raised his brows. "I'm sorry, but I wasn't aware that she was having nightmares. She never mentioned it."

"Well, she does. About being abducted."

"Ah. No, my bedroom is just across the hall, and I would've heard screaming."

Mrs. Cooper rubbed her forehead. "She was having them all summer. I'm relieved they've finally stopped. We were very worried about her."

"The police never caught the men who took her, or whoever hired them."

"I know." She sipped her coffee. "And what about this Shays fellow she talks about? Is he still harassing her?"

James wondered if he should tell Abby's mother about Shays's beating, and their visit from the police. He thought it best to let Abby decide how much to tell her parents.

"I think he's realizing that he's not going to drive Abby out of college. I wouldn't be surprised if he gives up."

Mrs. Cooper uttered a sigh of relief.

Abby appeared in the doorway and gave James the surprise of his life. The citified Abby in her long five-gored skirt and tailored shirtwaist had disappeared. In her place stood a no-nonsense ranch hand dressed to work.

He noticed her legs first. Who wouldn't? Those mile-high legs were fitted with a pair of faded, well-worn dungarees like her mother's.

James had never realized that Abigail Cooper possessed the longest pair of legs he'd ever seen. And hips that were anything but boyish.

He stared, transfixed. Why hadn't she told him that not only her mother wore pants in the Cooper family? Then he would have been prepared.

Abby had let down her hair and fashioned the glossy dark mane into one thick braid that hung down her back. She must have raided her father's dresser drawer, for she wore a man's shirt with the sleeves rolled up almost to her elbows. James was willing to bet his college tuition that she wore no corset under that shirt, either. He could see the outline of her round, full breasts.

She held him spellbound. Gone was the standoffish Ice Maiden, replaced by a warm, relaxed woman. A damn attractive woman.

He tore his eyes away and sipped his coffee before Abby's mother caught him ogling her daughter and got the wrong impression.

"Is the coffee still hot?" Abby headed for the stove, giving James an enticing view of her gently rounded backside.

"It should be," her mother replied.

Abby poured herself a cup and joined them at the table. "You all settled in?"

He nodded. With her hair pulled back, her eyes looked larger, like two serene blue pools.

"Would you like to see the rest of the farm?" she asked.

"I would."

"Good. As soon as we finish our coffee, I'll show you around."

11

THE MINUTE JAMES WALKED INTO THE SPACIOUS, spotless main barn with Abby, one horse neighed. Another answered from the opposite end of the barn. The bright-eyed chestnut in a box stall to their right stuck his head over the door and stared curiously before relaying his approval to the others.

"They're welcoming me home," Abby said as the equine symphony continued up and down the two rows of stalls. "At least I like to think that's what they're doing."

James thought of Moriarty's welcomes. The mastiff always bounded at him with unconditional acceptance and enthusiasm, his tail wagging excitedly.

He extended his hand so the horse could nuzzle his palm. "There's nothing like having someone who's happy to see you come home."

Abby gave him a quick questioning glance, but said nothing.

She walked from stall to stall, petting each horse and introducing it to James. Timber, Red Wind, old Rogue, Burgundy, Shooting Star . . . soon James's head was spinning from the effort to remember all the names Abby rattled off as effortlessly as old friends'.

"Is that you, puss?" called a hopeful masculine voice from the other end of the barn.

"Papa!" Abby cried, bolting off down the corridor.

James followed at a more sedate walk, petting some of the horses to allow father and daughter time for a more private reunion. When he caught up to Abby, she and her father were parting from a hug.

As Abby made the introductions, Michael Cooper extended his hand to James and gave him the same assessing, protective look as Abby's mother. "A pleasure."

They shook hands. "The pleasure's mine. And thank you for inviting me."

James thought that, aside from their similar dark coloring, Abby resembled her mother more than her father. But she did possess his straight nose and flaring brows.

"Papa," Abby said, frowning at a nearby empty stall, "where's Fireworks?"

"In the north field," he replied. "She was feeling her oats, so I had to let her out before she drove everybody else crazy with her snorting and stamping."

Abby turned to James, her face glowing with eagerness. "Let me say hello to my horse, and then we'll go riding, okay?" Before he could answer, she added, "I'm assuming that you *do* ride."

"Of course." He may have been raised in Chicago, but he'd learned to ride in England, and he enjoyed it.

"Good."

"I have work to do," Michael Cooper said, "so I'll see you two later." He placed a quick kiss on his daughter's forehead. "It's good to have you home, puss."

"It's good to be home," she replied.

James waited while Abby disappeared into the tack-room and emerged with a bridle. He followed her out of the barn and around the rear paddocks, where other horses, their usually glossy coats now thick and dull for winter, had churned up the light layer of snow and frozen earth into a quagmire of brown mud.

James kept stealing glances at Abby. She hadn't been home an hour, and already she'd shed her city skin like a butterfly its chrysalis. The serious, driven college student had remained behind at the train station. In her place strode a relaxed, lighthearted country girl.

This new and unexpected facet of her personality charmed and intrigued him. He wanted her to reveal more.

After passing several paddocks, they reached what must have been the north field.

Abby climbed on the high fence. "There she is."

At the far end of the field trotted a beautiful dappled gray mare so light on her feet she seemed to float over the ground.

James leaned against the weathered wood and rested his arms along the topmost rail. "Why'd you name her Fireworks?"

"Because she was born on Founders' Day, just when the fireworks went off. And, if you're not an experienced enough rider, she can be just as explosive."

Abby put her fingers up to her mouth and whistled.

Fireworks stopped and looked, her head up, her delicate ears pricked forward, her nostrils testing the air for a familiar scent.

Abby climbed over the fence and started walking toward her. James stayed behind.

Fireworks tossed her head with an impatient squeal

and broke into a canter, heading like a runaway train straight for Abby.

The ground shook.

James's heart stopped. "Abby."

She didn't move. "It's all right. She won't hurt me."

The charging mare veered away at the last minute with another playful toss of her head, turned in a wide circle, and came walking up to her smiling mistress. James let out a sigh of relief.

"You big baby," Abby crooned, extending her hand so the mare could nuzzle her gloved palm. "You scared James half to death with your wild-horse act, do you know that?"

With a veterinarian student's practiced eye, Abby quickly looked her over and nodded in satisfaction. "Papa's taken good care of you, girl. You're sleek and sound."

Fireworks snorted and tried to nibble on the end of Abby's braid.

"She's an Arabian, isn't she?" James asked, noticing the mare's delicate, sculpted face, arched neck, and lighter, more delicate build than most of the horses he'd seen today.

Abby nodded. "She's got Crabbet blood."

James knew from his summers in England that the Crabbet Stud bred the finest Arabian horses in the world. "I'm impressed."

"You should be." Abby stroked her horse's arched neck and bridled her. "Fireworks is a pretty impressive lady."

Abby took the reins, tangled the fingers of her left hand in the mane and placed her right hand on the mare's back. Fireworks rolled the bit between her teeth, but otherwise stood as still as a sculpture. Before James could protest, Abby sprang up and flung her right leg over the horse's back. She settled herself behind the withers, her long legs securely positioned behind the horse's shoulders.

An image of Abby dashed to the ground by a temperamental, unpredictable horse flashed through James's mind.

He gripped the fence. "Get down," he said softly. "Now."

Abby looked at him as if he'd lost his mind. "I ride bareback all the time."

Bareback. No saddle, no stirrups. Only a bridle to control the horse's head.

"Abby . . ."

The headstrong Miss Cooper suddenly went deaf. Abby touched her heels to the mare's sides. With a sassy flip of her long tail, Fireworks walked a few steps before her rider urged her into a smooth trot.

James fought the urge to climb over the fence and pull Abby down off that horse before she broke her fool neck. Yet the spirited Arabian settled down immediately, obeying Abby's every command as if she were a docile puppy.

He'd never seen anyone ride like Abby. She seemed to melt like soft candle wax into her mount, so that James couldn't determine where the horse left off and the rider began.

Abby reached the far end of the field. She turned Fireworks, bent low over the horse's neck, and gave a verbal command.

The mare broke from a standstill into a canter. Even the thrust of a forward charge didn't unseat Abby. She stuck to that horse's bare back like a burr.

She thundered toward him, perfectly balanced and at

one with her mount, an exultant grin on her face. She looked so happy, so content, that James couldn't help smiling.

She halted Fireworks beside the fence and slid off her back. Abby's cheeks were flushed, and she glowed.

Abby gave the mare an affectionate slap on the neck. "Isn't she wonderful?"

"Yes." But he wasn't referring to the horse.

"Would you like to go riding now?" she asked. "I can show you the rest of the farm, and then we can ride over to my grandfather Jace's place. If you think the Cooper horses are outstanding, you should see my grandfather's stock."

"I'd like that."

Abby led her horse out of the field and back to the barn, so she and James could saddle up and take their ride.

James stood in the darkness of his bedroom and stared out the window at the clear night sky. The spray of stars seemed to twinkle. He seldom saw stars this bright in the city.

He listened. All he heard was footsteps, followed by a door closing down the hall. Then silence. He looked down into the yard. No furtive figures lurked in the shadow of the barn.

He closed his eyes and let the peace enfold him.

He had traveled a long, long way from Nick's dark, dangerous underworld, and not just in miles.

James crossed his arms, leaned against the windowsill and stared at the moon. He envied Abby's hard-working parents and grandparents their good, decent, uncompli-cated life. They welcomed him into their home as if he were family. At dinner, they did their best to put him at ease and to banish the awkwardness that always rose between strangers struggling to find some common ground. They conversed, but never pried.

Nick's world intruded only once.

After supper, they retired to the parlor, where Abby and her father played checkers, James read a veterinary journal, and Mrs. Cooper darned socks.

"Abby," her mother said, "I hope that Shays fellow has finally stopped harassing you."

James stopped reading, but he didn't look up and catch Abby's eye. He held his breath, waiting for her to tell her parents that someone had beaten up Shays, and that the police suspected, but couldn't prove, she and James had something to do with it.

He heard her say, "Oh, he stopped when James moved into the boardinghouse and started escorting me to school."

Now he looked up. Why didn't she tell her parents the truth?

Mrs. Cooper beamed at him. "So we've you to thank for protecting our daughter."

"I owe you one, son," her husband added. "I've been of half a mind to go to Chicago myself and beat some sense into that Shays fellow. But my wife takes exception to violence."

"I wouldn't want any harm to come to you, Michael," his wife replied. "You're not a young buck anymore."

Her husband grunted.

"I wish I could've done more," James said. And sooner. If only he didn't fear the dark places in his own soul, and unleashing his own demons.

After Abby's father narrowly beat his daughter at checkers, conversation turned to Abby's youngest sister,

Lizzie, the artist, due to arrive from San Francisco late the next afternoon. Then everyone retired for the night.

James looked out the window across the serene landscape touched with silver moonlight. He wondered what Abby would say if he told her about Nick.

He rubbed his jaw. He really didn't want to find out.

Abby awoke at nine o'clock the following morning, rushed to wash and dress, then went downstairs for breakfast.

She kissed her mother on the cheek and reached for the coffee pot. "Where is everybody?"

"Everybody is working, puss," her mother replied with an indulgent smile. "Everyone except citified sleepyheads." She broke several eggs into a bowl, then fished out small pieces of shell with a spoon. "James came down at the crack of dawn and offered to help your father feed the horses and muck out stalls." She scrambled the eggs with a fork. "We like him. He seems like such a fine, upstanding young man."

"He is." Abby set the bread to toast, then added butter to the hot cast-iron fry pan, and proceeded to cook her breakfast.

"What do you have planned for today?" Cat asked.

Abby brought her plate over to the stove and served herself. "I thought I'd ride into town." To see Kyle.

"I'm sure James would like to meet your grandmother and sister."

"Actually, since he's busy with Papa, I thought I'd go alone."

Cat frowned. "Abigail Cooper, you know better than to leave a guest to go gallivanting."

Abby sighed. Only her mother could make her feel like an ill-mannered eight-year-old with dirt on her chin.

"I do know better, Mother, but somehow, I don't think James will mind. He's going to be a vet. He likes being around horses."

"If you're going into town, at least make sure you see your grandmother and sister. They'll be very hurt if you don't."

"I will." She always enjoyed Grandmama Maddy's company, especially her endlessly entertaining stories of life when she was a girl, but she could only tolerate so much of Regina's rampaging self-centeredness.

After wolfing down her breakfast, Abby said good-bye to her mother, and headed for the barn.

She found her father and James still working.

James grinned like a little boy standing in a mud puddle. "Grab a pitchfork and dig in."

"Much as I love to clean stalls, I planned to ride into town today. Care to join me?" She mentally crossed her fingers, hoping he'd refuse.

James stopped and leaned against his pitchfork. "Your father has kindly agreed to let me practice my veterinary skills on his horses."

Abby raised her brows. Her father allowed only his wife and daughter to examine and treat his beloved horses.

He must really like James, she thought. It annoyed her that he had never appeared as at ease with Kyle.

"Then he's going along with me to examine your grandfather's stock," her father added. "So it looks like you're on your own for the day, puss."

"Then I'll see you later," she said, and went off to saddle Fireworks.

When Abby arrived in town, she went to her grand-mother's house first. Since Grandmama Maddy insisted on hearing the latest news about Abby's studies and Josie's life, Abby made them tea, and they sat at the kitchen table and caught up for several hours.

During the course of their conversation, Abby's grandmother asked question after question about James Bradshaw, until Abby laughingly asked her if she was playing matchmaker. Only then did Maddy change the subject, reminding Abby once more that Kyle had bid on Mary Dobbs's box lunch.

After Abby left, she went to the Dobbs Mercantile to buy some lemon drops for her mother. The mercantile had been established before the Civil War by Mary's grandfather Festus, who now did nothing more strenuous than stock the shelves when he felt like it, preferring to let his son and granddaughter run the business. Not only did Festus bequeath the mercantile to his progeny, he passed on his unfortunate looks as well.

Buxom eighteen-year-old Mary waited on her.

"So when are you and Kyle getting married?" Mary said, opening the candy jar and scooping some lemon drops into a small paper bag. One of the buttons on her strained bodice popped, but she ignored it. Mary's buttons were always popping, much to the delight of half the male population.

"Sometime in June, after I graduate," Abby replied. "We haven't set a date yet."

"You're lucky." The colorless Mary sighed wistfully. "He's a real nice man."

"I think so."

"Lots of folks do." She held up the bag. "This enough?"

"Another scoop, please," Abby said. "I understand you shared your box lunch with him at the Harvest Festival."

Mary's pale, protruding eyes suddenly hardened with

pent-up resentment, whether toward Kyle or men in general Abby couldn't tell. "I know he only bid on it because nobody else did. But afterward, he admitted he was glad he did, because," she added proudly, "he said he enjoyed my company."

"I'm sure he did." Abby took the proffered bag. "You're a nice girl, too, Mary."

Mary stared at her as though this was the first compliment she'd ever received in her life. She said nothing, just took Abby's money and gave her back change.

After leaving the mercantile, Abby stopped at the post office to pick up the mail, then went on to One-Eyed Jack's.

"Where's Kyle?" she said to Minnie, who was industriously sweeping the floor.

"In his office."

Abby went around to the back room at the end of a long, narrow corridor. She knocked, and when he said, "Come in," she opened the door to find him seated at his desk, papers spread out all around him.

"You busy?" she asked. "If you are, I'll come back later."

His swivel chair creaked as he swung around and let out a low appreciative whistle when he noticed she was wearing her dungarees. "Never too busy for you, honey, especially when you look like that." He rose. "Close that door and come here." He checked into the hallway beyond. "Unless, of course, your friend Bradshaw is with you."

Abby closed the door, set down her parcels, and unbuttoned her jacket. "I'm alone this time."

"Good." He took her coat and hung it on a hook behind the door. "I don't like sharing you with anybody.'' He turned back and pulled her into his arms for a kiss.

When they parted, Kyle grinned in masculine satisfaction. ''Nobody kisses like you, Abby. Your lips are sweeter than sugar and honey combined.''

Abby smiled back. ''So are yours. Not that I've ever kissed anyone else to compare, mind you.''

''Good thing.'' He indicated the chair near his desk. ''I assume you're here to discuss wedding plans, so have a seat.'' His swivel chair squeaked as he lowered his tall frame into it.

Abby sat down. ''Before we discuss wedding plans . . . why didn't you tell me that you bid on Mary Dobbs's box lunch when nobody else would? I had to hear about it from my grandmother.''

Kyle squirmed and averted his eyes. ''I wasn't trying to hide anything from you, I just didn't think it worth mentioning, that's all. I know we're courting, but you weren't at the Harvest Festival, and there was homely Mary, so embarrassed, and trying so hard not to cry.'' He shrugged. ''I felt sorry for her.''

''I don't mind.'' Abby's heart swelled with emotion. ''When I heard what you'd done, I felt so proud.''

''Oh, go on, Abby, don't make so much of this. I didn't do anything special, just spent a few hours in Mary's company.''

''Well, it was special to her,'' Abby said. ''I just came from the mercantile, and I can tell you that you really made an impression on her.''

''Actually, she may not be the prettiest girl in the world, but she has quite a head for business. Most people take one look at her face and act like she's not there. But for all intents and purposes, she runs that mercantile herself. I spent a good part of that lunch listening to her tell me what I could do to increase the saloon's profits."

Abby raised her brows. "Should I be jealous?"

Kyle threw back his head and laughed. "Not even a little bit, honey. You've got a head for business yourself—veterinary business—*and* you're the prettiest girl in the world."

"Then the wedding's still on."

Kyle reached for his calendar. "Why don't we set a date? The sooner the better."

"How about the last Saturday in June?" Abby suggested.

"The twenty-fifth." Kyle ran his hand through his golden hair, tousling it. "Perfect." He reached for his pencil and circled the date. "Not that I won't remember the most important date of my life."

June twenty-fifth, the day Abigail Cooper would become Mrs. Kyle Lambert.

"So much to do," Abby said. "I'll have to have my wedding dress made, and dresses for Lizzie and Regina. We have to decide whom to invite. Where to go on our honeymoon."

Kyle frowned thoughtfully. "We're going to have to find a place to live. The saloon here is fine for a single gent, but not a married man with a wife."

"And children," Abby added. "Let's not forget them."

"Don't put the cart before the horse, honey. Let's get married and settled first before we start thinking about little ones."

"Well, I know I want them, even if it will be hard to combine raising them with my veterinary career. Up until now, I assumed you did, too." She smiled. "I just needed to know for sure."

Kyle tapped his chin with his pencil. "Why don't we

build a nice big house at the other end of Main Street, near Regina? That way, we'll have plenty of room for those children we want, and they'll have their little cousins right next door to play with."

"We don't have enough money to build a house," Abby said. "I was thinking that since Dr. Kendall will be retiring as soon as I hang out my shingle, and since my Grandpapa Boswell owns the surgery building, why don't we live upstairs over my veterinary surgery?"

"Now, why didn't I think of that? Like I said, honey, you have a head for business that puts Mary's to shame."

"Or we could live in the boardinghouse. I know my grandmother would love the company."

"Much as I love and respect your grandmother," Kyle said, giving Abby a smoldering look, "I think newlyweds ought to have a little privacy. Hell, a *lot* of privacy. I want to have my new bride all to myself."

Her heart swelled with love. "How was I so lucky to find the perfect man?"

"I'm the lucky one. I found the perfect woman." He made a few notes, then leaned back in his chair. "Do you know what your parents are planning to give us as a wedding present?"

Abby shook her head. "They haven't told me."

Kyle rose and went over to the window overlooking the alley. With his back to Abby, he said, "I really feel like a snake bringing this up, honey, but"—he turned to face her—"do you think your parents would consider buying us the saloon as a wedding present?"

Before Abby could reply, Kyle strode over to her and grasped her hands. "It wouldn't be just for me, it would be for us, and our future. And the future of our children."

He held her hands tightly, and there was a desperate glint in the depths of his blue eyes. Abby knew how much he wanted to buy his boss out and be his own man. She also knew what it cost him to swallow his pride and ask this of her. Kyle Lambert didn't like to ask a favor of anyone.

"You know how much I want you to have Jack's," she said soothingly, "but I'd feel really funny asking my parents for anything. They've already paid for my education."

Kyle sighed. "I don't mean to put you in the middle. It's just that once I own the saloon, I can get rid of the girls and run a more respectable establishment. I can prove to your family that I'm worthy of marrying their daughter."

Abby rose and placed a hand against his cheek. "Don't worry. Everything will work out."

"I just want to make all your dreams come true," he said.

She kissed him. "You will."

12

❦

At THE SOUND OF HOOFBEATS AND DOGS BARKING, Abby bolted out of her chair and ran to the parlor window.

"Lizard's here!" she cried.

James raised his brows as he looked across the checkerboard at Michael Cooper. "Lizard?"

Abby's father rose, just as eager as his wife and daughter to welcome his youngest child home. "She didn't tell you that's what she usually calls Lizzie?"

James smiled and rose. "That's original, if not exactly complimentary."

"I can tell you don't have any sisters," Cooper said, heading for the door.

"Not a one," James replied. Thank God Nick Flynn never had a daughter. A man had it hard enough growing up with the constant companions of danger and fear.

"Neither do I. As a man who's raised three daughters, I can tell you firsthand that their bond is truly a mystery."

James walked out onto the porch with Cooper and waited with him while Abby and her mother went to welcome Lizzie, who'd driven a rented buggy out to the farm.

After Abby and her mother had hugged Lizzie nearly to death, they marched back to the house, chattering all at once like birds before a thunderstorm. How was her train ride across half the country? Did she enjoy school? How long was she staying? On and on.

When Lizzie saw her father standing on the porch, she shouted, ''Papa!'' and ran the rest of the way with all the dignity of a schoolgirl.

James hung back in the shadows as a tall, red-headed woman flung herself into her father's arms for a joyful reunion.

Abby hurried up the steps to stand by James's side. ''Lizzie, this is James Bradshaw, a classmate of mine. I invited him to spend Christmas with us.''

Lizzie sized him up before welcoming him to the Cooper farm. She and James exchanged pleasantries, then Mrs. Cooper ushered everyone inside and left them catching up in the parlor while she made coffee.

Once everyone held a cup, Abby pressed Lizzie to show some examples of her work. The minute Lizzie took a sketchbook out of her bag, Abby brought it over to show James.

''Wait until you see these,'' she said, taking the chair next to him. She looked over at Lizzie, and said, ''Hard to believe my baby Lizard is so talented,'' loud enough for her sister to hear.

Lizzie promptly stuck out her tongue. Abby retaliated like any self-respecting four-year-old.

James opened the bound sketchbook, but found he couldn't concentrate on masterful, evocative watercolors of the sun-washed California landscape, or the deft, dramatic pen-and-ink portraits. Abby clouded his mind.

She kept leaning closer and closer to him and craning her neck so that she could see the pictures as he turned each page. Her arm pressed against his. James could have pulled away, but he didn't. He turned another page, trying to ignore the fact that her pale cheek, with its thin white scar from Shays's snowball, was close enough to kiss. And why hadn't he ever noticed her scent before, the fresh, clean fragrance of a flower-filled English meadow after a light summer sprinkle? Even when he'd carried her back to the boardinghouse after her injury, he hadn't noticed her subtle perfume. Probably because they'd just come from the clinic, with its overpowering animal odors. Now that he had noticed her unique fragrance, he found that it lingered in his mind, like a song overheard.

His gaze slid from the sketchbook to Abby's long denim-sheathed crossed legs. The effect was anything but mannish. James pulled his enthralled gaze back to the sketchbook. Fast, before anyone noticed. Good thing the sketchbook covered his lap, or he'd embarrass himself.

"I especially like that drawing of Fireworks," Abby said, her warm, coffee-scented breath brushing his cheek.

"Your sister has captured her spirit so perfectly," he said, "that she looks ready to come alive."

So did Abby. The loving, easygoing family atmosphere of the Cooper farm had melted the Ice Maiden's stone-cold heart. Ever since coming to Little Falls, James had discovered that Abby Cooper could be kind and compassionate. She radiated contentment and happiness. This was where she belonged, not some dirty, bustling big city.

He belonged here, too.

With her.

The overwhelming attraction he felt for Abby hit him like an arrow straight through the heart. He sat there, stunned, while she flipped to another sketch of her horse.

First they'd been adversaries, then friends. Now his feelings had transformed into much more than friendship. A stronger emotion that he was powerless to control tugged at both his mind and his heart.

He realized that until now, he'd only half existed, a puzzle seeking some nameless piece that would complete the picture that defined his existence. Abby supplied that piece.

Unfortunately, she'd already found her other half with Kyle Lambert.

Later that night, after the yawning Cooper household had retired, Abby sat cross-legged at the foot of Lizzie's bed while her sister sat at her dressing table and brushed her auburn curls until they crackled.

"It's good to have you home," she said. "I've missed you something fierce."

Lizzie turned and smiled. "I've missed you, too, Doc. Letters just aren't the same as sitting here in person." Her freckled face turned wistful. "California is such a long way from Little Falls, I can't take the train home every time I feel like it."

"But you like it out there, don't you?"

"I do. Oh, I get homesick sometimes, but the city is filled with such energy. The weather is so sunny and warm. I'm learning so much in school." She beamed. "My teachers think I have real artistic talent."

"Well, that's obvious."

"Denny and Ruby couldn't be nicer if they were my own parents." She wrinkled her pert nose. "Though never having had any brothers, I could cheerfully smother the boys a hundred times a day."

Denny Dunleavy, a talented photographer who'd once lived in the boardinghouse when Abby's own mother ran it many years ago, and his wife, Ruby, had two sons close to Lizzie's age. They'd graciously offered to let Lizzie live with them while she attended art school. Otherwise her parents would never have allowed her to go to California.

Lizzie stopped brushing and leaned forward. She glanced at the door as if expecting their mother to listen in at the keyhole. Then she lowered her voice to a stage whisper. "Guess what I found out?"

Abby leaned forward and whispered back, "Oh, goody, a secret. Tell me, tell me."

Lizzie looked as if she could hardly contain herself. "Papa and Mrs. Dunleavy were once lovers."

Abby's eyes widened in shock, and her jaw dropped. "Papa and Ruby? I don't believe it. Elizabeth Ellen Cooper, you're making this up."

"I am not!"

"Swear on Zeke's grave," Abby demanded, referring to Grandmama Maddy's beloved coonhound buried beneath the sycamore where he had treed the first in a long line of cats named Ulysses. She knew that the sacred childhood oath would force Lizzie to tell the truth.

Lizzie placed her right hand over her heart. "I, Elizabeth Ellen Cooper, solemnly swear on Zeke's grave that Papa and Ruby were once lovers."

"But—but she was a *saloon girl*!" She'd only met Ruby Dunleavy twice in her life, when the family came out to Little Falls to visit, but she liked her, as did Lizzie. "Men paid her to . . ." Her voice trailed off.

Lizzie shrugged and resumed brushing with long, relentless strokes. "This was in his wilder, younger days, of course," she added, "long before he fell in love with Mama."

Abby rocked back. "I don't believe it. Papa and Ruby. Who told you?"

"Their eldest son. Don't ask me how he found out, because he wouldn't tell me. I believe him, though." Lizzie frowned at her. "You're not going to go all priggish on me about this, are you, Abigail, and tell Papa that I told you?"

"I just think it's very hypocritical of Papa to suspect Kyle of paying upstairs visits to the girls when he himself did the same with Ruby."

"Men have two standards, one for themselves and one for their daughters. You know that. He just wants to protect you from heartache." Lizzie scowled at her. "You'd better promise you won't tell him, or I'll never share another secret with you as long as I live."

Abby sniffed. "I won't say a word. You're not the only one who's so sophisticated, you know."

Lizzie giggled and tossed the hairbrush at Abby, missing her by an intended mile. Abby grabbed a pillow and flung it at Lizzie, who caught it and threw it back.

"Shhh! Not so loud," Abby warned, just before the pillow hit her in the head. "We'll wake everyone up."

Lizzie glanced at the door. "I'm surprised Mother hasn't come by to tell us lights out."

"We're not children anymore, that's why." Abby plucked at the lace on her nightgown's sleeve. "Do you think Mama knows about Papa and Ruby?"

"I'm sure she does."

"You're right. They don't keep secrets from each other." Abby shook her head in disbelief. "A *saloon girl* . . ."

Lizzie pulled back her hair and tied it with a ribbon. "Kyle works with such women every day. Doesn't that upset you? I know it'd upset me."

"For the millionth time, Kyle doesn't own Jack's, he only runs it. The owner insists that he keep the girls because they increase revenue. Once Kyle saves enough money to buy Jack's, he's going to get rid of the girls."

Lizzie climbed onto the bed, pulled her nightgown down to cover her knees, and sat facing Abby. "That's very admirable."

"Kyle's an admirable man."

Lizzie settled herself more comfortably on the bed. "I know this very wise Chinese woman who once told me that in every couple's life, they bring each other special gifts. Sometimes this gift is an occurrence that makes one of them realize that they love the other. At other times, the gifts come much later in life, bringing other messages or lessons.

"I was thinking about that on the train ride out here. Do you remember Grandmama Maddy telling us about the time Grandpapa Paul saved Zeke when he became paralyzed?"

"Of course I do." Her grandmother was about to shoot her helpless dog, when she realized that perhaps Dr. Paul Wills's knowledge of modern veterinary medicine just might save the coonhound's life. When Dr. Paul Wills performed that miracle, he won Maddy's heart.

"That was our grandfather's gift to her," Lizzie said softly. "Just as our own father gave Mama the gift of her reputation as a vet when he exposed Dr. Kendall for spreading lies about Mama's competency."

"Your point, Lizard?"

"What such gift has Kyle given to you?"

"Kyle is always giving me gifts," Abby retorted. "Flowers, candy, books of poetry."

"Those aren't the kinds of gifts I'm talking about, and you know it."

"He's given me the gift of his love." When Lizzie made no comment, Abby said, "Why do you object to my marrying Kyle? I know our parents don't approve of him because they think he's paying secret upstairs visits to the girls. What's your reason?"

"I just think you could find someone better, that's all. Someone of similar intellect and passions."

"Kyle's not stupid."

"I didn't say he was." Lizzie sighed. "I don't see you and Kyle as a couple, the way I see Mama and Papa together, or our grandparents."

"I'm sorry you feel that way. Maybe it's time we talked about something else."

Lizzie smiled. "Why don't we discuss this Mr. Bradshaw of yours?"

"He's not *my* anything."

"Too bad. I've only just met him and I don't know him very well, but I really like him."

Abby smiled sweetly. "He's not married. Or even seeing anyone."

Lizzie raised her pale reddish brows. "Are all the women in Chicago blind?"

"Those of us who already have men of our own."

Lizzie leaned back against the iron headboard. "Now, there's a man with secrets."

That observation took Abby aback. "Why would you think that?"

"We artists can always tell, my dear. We train ourselves to look beyond the facade our subjects present to the world. We dig to get under their skin to capture their essence on paper or canvas, to—''

''Lizzie.''

''Sorry. I didn't mean to gush on about the philosophy of art to you, pragmatic scientist that you are. There's just something about his eyes, a haunted quality I can't explain.''

''I don't know him very well, but he's always struck me as intensely private.''

''As I said, a man with deep, dark secrets.'' She hugged her pillow. ''Do you think he'd let me sketch him? In the nude?''

Abby blushed furiously when she visualized a naked James Bradshaw posing for her sister. She cleared her throat. ''Somehow, I think that our parents would object.''

Lizzie sighed. ''But I can tell he'd be such a perfect subject. That black, windswept hair, that handsome, brooding face . . . those broad, muscular shoulders.'' She licked her lower lip as if about to sample a tasty dish. ''I'll bet without his clothes, he'd put Michelangelo's *David* to shame.''

Abby raised a wry, mocking brow. ''When James Bradshaw takes off his clothes in a woman's presence, I suspect it's not to pose for his portrait.''

Lizzie grinned wickedly. ''I'm willing to find out.''

An unexpected bolt of raw emotion startled Abby. ''Elizabeth Ellen Cooper, just get that indecent thought right out of your head.''

''A man that handsome and mysterious inspires indecent thoughts.'' Lizzie propped her elbow on one knee and cradled her chin in her palm. She drummed her fingertips against her cheek. ''Have you noticed his sensuous, sculpted lips? I'll bet when he kisses, he—''

"Okay, Lizzie, lights out."

"Spoilsport!"

Abby stifled a yawn and climbed off the bed. "That's what big sisters are for." She walked up to Lizzie and gave her a hug. "Welcome home, little Lizard. Thanks for the sisterly chat and unwanted advice. See you in the morning."

"G'night," Lizzie whispered, crawling beneath the covers and drawing them up to her chin. She shivered. "I'm freezing. It's never this cold in California."

Abby took the lamp from the dressing table and headed for the door. "You'll get used to it."

Lizzie grinned at her sister's teasing. "Sleep tight, Doc."

But when Abby returned to her own room and got into bed, sleep was the furthest thing from her mind.

She lay there staring at the ceiling, unable to think of anything except Lizzie's admiring and suggestive comments about James. His windswept hair, his handsome, brooding face, his sensuous, sculpted mouth . . .

Had Lizzie been serious about approaching James to pose for her? Abby dashed that thought right out of her head. Lizzie would never be able to get away with it. Not in her parents' home, anyway. But what if she found somewhere secluded and private, where she and James would be undisturbed?

She wouldn't dare, Abby thought.

And then she put a name to the unsettling emotion that she'd been experiencing ever since Lizzie mentioned painting a nude James Bradshaw.

Jealousy.

Later the following morning, after halfheartedly helping Abby's father with the chores, James discovered he had the house to himself, so he took his surgical procedures textbook into the parlor to study.

The words turned into a blur on the page. Evocative thoughts of Abby marred his ability to concentrate. He kept seeing her smile and hearing her laugh.

He'd known other women. Nick had seen to it that his son had been initiated into the pleasures of the boudoir at an early age. James had been an apt pupil. But he'd never been the kind of man who could separate the act itself from the woman. He always demanded something more. Intelligent conversation. A revelation of hopes and dreams. He found the sharing of minds enhanced the sharing of bodies. Consequently, he was very discerning in his choice of bed partners.

He knew that if he ever got Abby into bed, he'd never want her to leave.

He closed his eyes and rubbed his face. He ached to get her alone somewhere, pull her into his arms and kiss her. Really kiss her. He'd start slowly, holding her tenderly, letting her adjust to the feeling of being in his arms. When she surrendered and accepted him, he'd deepen his kisses. He could hear her little moan of surrender, feel her quiver and melt in his arms. And then . . .

He opened his eyes and swore. She loved Kyle Lambert. Unlike Nick, James wouldn't try to take what belonged to another.

He returned to his studying. This time, the words made perfect sense.

No sooner did he finish reading the first page when the front door opened and Lizzie Cooper came whirling in like the Chicago wind, a sketch pad tucked under one arm, and a box of paints in the other hand.

James smiled and rose to take them from her. "Been painting?"

"As much as I was able in this cold," she replied, pulling off her hat and unwinding her long scarf. "Would you like to see?"

"I would."

Ever since meeting the artistic Cooper sister yesterday, James knew he'd have to be careful around her. Lizzie studied everything from objects to people with penetrating intensity. She probed. She analyzed. She exposed.

In spite of the danger, he liked her. She displayed warmth, friendliness, and unlike her sister Regina, an utter lack of conceit.

He helped her out of her coat. "Where are your dungarees? I thought all the Cooper women wore them when they rode."

Lizzie made a face as if she'd stepped in a mile of horse manure. "Dungarees? I wouldn't be caught dead in those hideous things. And as for riding, I wouldn't be caught dead doing that either. I can't abide horses, except to paint." She shuddered. "Big, scary, smelly animals."

James smiled. "You're a disgrace to your family."

"I just march to the beat of a different drummer," she replied. "I always have."

He could well believe it. "I noticed you not only sign your work with your name, but you paint a little black lizard beneath it." He hung up her coat and turned. "Like James McNeill Whistler's signature butterfly."

She looked surprised. "You know something about artists, I see."

"When I lived in England, I knew several. One of them was a friend of Whistler's."

Lizzie's green eyes nearly popped out of her head, and her jaw dropped. "You knew someone who knew Whistler?"

He nodded.

"I am impressed."

He didn't think it prudent to tell her that he sometimes watched John Singer Sargent paint his mother's portrait. The poor girl would have swooned in ecstasy.

"You're a man of many surprises, James," she said, opening her pad.

"So I've been told."

"By my sister, I'm sure."

He merely smiled and let her draw her own conclusions.

They sat down together on the sofa, and Lizzie opened her sketch pad. The barn, the house, and a group of horses standing idly in a field all came to life in the finely detailed watercolors.

"You're an exceptional artist," James said.

She beamed and thanked him. She closed the pad, set it aside, and faced him directly, a serious expression on her pretty face. "James, I'd like you to do me a favor."

"What kind of favor?"

"I'd like you to come between Abby and Kyle Lambert."

13

HOPE SURGED THROUGH HIM. HE DASHED IT AT once.

"Miss Cooper, are you out of your mind?"

"I assure you, I'm dead serious," Lizzie replied. "I'm asking—no, begging—you to come between my sister and Kyle. Not forever. Just for a little while."

"Abby and I have no romantic feelings for each other. Most of the time I've known her, we've been adversaries. It's only just recently that she's begun to trust me, and regard me as a friend."

Lizzie bobbed her head. "That's good. Now all you have to do is pretend to be infatuated with her. She'll realize that she doesn't love Kyle and break it off with him. Once that happens, you can tell her that your infatuation for her has died, and—" Lizzie groaned. "This isn't going to work, is it?"

He smiled wryly. "If you were a race horse, I wouldn't bet on you."

She hung her head. "It was a harebrained idea, and I'm thoroughly ashamed of myself."

"I realize you're desperate to keep Abby from marrying this man, but I couldn't be a party to such a scheme. I respect and admire her too much to deliberately fool her.''

Lizzie sighed. "It was just a thought.''

"Even if I did go along with you, I wouldn't have any time to convince her of my infatuation. Tomorrow is Christmas, the day Kyle is going to give her a ring.'' He shook his head. "I'm afraid your sister's made her choice.''

"She's making a terrible mistake.''

"Why do you think that? I've only met him once, but Lambert seems decent enough. Very hardworking, and successful.''

She curled her lip. "He's about as exciting as watching milk curdle. My sister needs a man who'll challenge her intellect, who shares her passion for animals, who'll put her happiness above his own.''

"And you don't think Lambert is that man?''

"Do you?''

"No.'' But not for the reasons she thought. He closed his textbook. "She's not married yet. A lot can happen in five months to change her mind.''

Lizzie drummed her fingertips against her cheek. "Once Abby's mind is made up, she never changes it.''

James smiled. "She may surprise you.''

Lizzie rose and gathered her art supplies. "Thank you for your compliments about my paintings. I do apologize for trying to drag you into our little family drama. I can see that you'd have no part in such a deception.''

"I won't hold it against you.'' James rose. "You only care about your sister.''

"If you'll excuse me, I have more painting to do.''

After Lizzie left the parlor, James picked up his textbook and tried to resume studying, but found he couldn't concentrate, a lamentable state that had afflicted him ever since he admitted to himself his attraction to Abby. He gave up, closed his book, and set it aside.

He shouldn't have been surprised by the lengths to which Lizzie Cooper had been prepared to go to save her sister. Devotion and protectiveness ran as deep and pure as a vein of gold in some families. Even Nick possessed it, in a dark and twisted way.

James wondered why Lizzie thought that he could possibly be a threat to Kyle Lambert.

Yet here she was, ready to throw him into Abby's arms at the drop of a hat. Couldn't she see that, even if he was unprincipled enough to go along with her harebrained scheme, her sister would surely rebuff his advances?

He rose and went to the window. He watched as Abby and her mother came walking from the stableyard toward the house. Mrs. Cooper was talking and gesturing about something, and Abby kept nodding and smiling in agreement.

She radiated such joy that James felt his heart turn over. He wished now that he'd sought her out that first day of veterinarian school. At the time, he'd been too preoccupied with his own studies. Perhaps if he'd gotten to know Abby sooner, she wouldn't be getting engaged to Lambert tomorrow.

He pushed the bittersweet regret aside, and went to open the front door.

"Time to open the presents," Mrs. Cooper announced after everyone finished Christmas dinner and the table had been cleared. "Everyone into the parlor."

James watched as Abby exchanged a long, melting look with Kyle, who'd sat so close to her during Christmas dinner that a knife blade couldn't have been inserted between them. In a few minutes, he would present her with a ring, and they would be officially engaged.

The saloon keeper looked as proud of himself as Nick did when his horses won at the track. He leaned over and whispered something into Abby's ear that made her blush.

Damn him.

Maddy placed an age-spotted hand over James's. "I'd like you to escort me into the parlor."

Abby's grandfather, Jace, seated at Maddy's right, looked at her with chagrin. "Hey, Red, I thought I'd be the one to escort you, seeing as how we're the grandparents."

"This is one time you're not going to get the girl, Jace Cooper," Maddy said. "James here is younger and better looking."

"I may be younger," James said, "but I don't know about better looking."

For a man in his midseventies, Jason Cooper was a fine, rugged figure of a man, with mischievous blue eyes that even the loss of his wife couldn't dim, and a roguish, lopsided smile that still charmed the pants off the ladies of any age.

Jace grinned. "I like you, Bradshaw. Not only are you a first-class vet, you're a gentleman."

James rose and held Maddy's chair. When she stepped away from the table, he offered his arm.

The rest of the family waited for Maddy to lead the way, as befitted her position as matriarch of the Cooper clan. Maddy didn't sit on the sofa, as James thought she would, but selected a chair in an out-of-the-way corner.

"Pull up a chair right next to me," she said.

James did as he was told.

Once everyone found a seat, the women of the family started distributing gifts that had been piled beneath the tree. Soon the room was abuzz with chatter.

''I think Lizzie most resembles me, don't you think?'' Maddy whispered.

''She has your fiery hair and green eyes,'' James agreed, ''but I think Abby has more of your spirit.''

Maddy looked quite pleased with his assessment. ''I've always thought that myself.''

Regina interrupted their conversation by handing her grandmother two boxes, then she went back to the tree and scolded her little daughter, Katie, for attempting to open a box that didn't belong to her.

''When Cat told me that Abby was bringing a strange man home for Christmas,'' Maddy said, ''I wondered if she'd found another sweetheart.''

James squirmed under the old lady's scrutiny. ''We're just good friends.''

''Good friends!'' Maddy sputtered. ''Are you blind? My granddaughter is beautiful. Smart, too. She'll make the right man a fine wife.''

''I know she will,'' James whispered back. ''She's also engaged to Kyle. Even if I did have romantic feelings toward Abby, I wouldn't try to take what belongs to another man.''

Maddy rolled her eyes. ''If a smart, good-looking fellow like you can't turn her head and make her forget a smooth talker like Lambert, then my Abby has a stone for a heart and feathers for brains.'' She shook her head. ''And with you two living together.''

James prayed that Abby's father hadn't overheard that remark. He wagged a reproachful finger at Maddy. ''No more matchmaking. You don't know me. I could be a ruthless criminal.'' Or the son of one.

"My granddaughter wouldn't have asked you to meet her family if she didn't hold you in high regard," Maddy pointed out. "Besides, I've become a good judge of character in my old age. I think you're a fine, upstanding young man."

James found Maddy's faith in him, a complete stranger she'd known so briefly, both touching and humbling. "I don't know what to say."

The old lady studied him out of those sharp, shrewd green eyes that saw far too much. "What if you did have romantic feelings for her? What would you do if she felt the same way?"

"Maddy . . ."

"Come, come." She leaned forward, and her eyes held a challenging glint. "What are you afraid of?"

He was spared replying by Lizzie, who suddenly separated herself from the rest of the crowd and approached them.

"What are you two whispering about in the corner?" She handed James a flat, brightly wrapped package. "You have to open this right away. It's from Abby and me."

James felt all eyes on him as he tore the paper. "I wonder what this could be?"

The small, framed watercolor depicted the Cooper farm as it must look in the summer, the fields lush and green, the skies blue and cloudless, with horses grazing in the foreground.

"Something to remember us by," Abby said from across the room.

He looked around the room so fast it blurred. "As if I could ever forget the Cooper farm. Or the people who make it so special."

The room fell silent. Mrs. Cooper looked at her husband and smiled. Abby regarded him with a wistful expression.

Jace flashed his lopsided grin. "Well said, son."

Conversation resumed, accompanied by the sound of ribbons snapping, paper tearing, and exclamations of delight and gratitude. Regina gasped when she opened the box containing a double-strand pearl necklace from her banker husband. Little Katie's eyes grew wide when she opened a doll with a porcelain head, real hair, and wearing a green velvet dress trimmed with lace.

James watched as Abby opened one gift after another until only one remained. His gift.

When she read the tag, she looked up at him in surprise. "You didn't have to get me anything."

No, he didn't, but he'd wanted to the minute he'd seen it in the shop window.

"I hope you like it."

She unwrapped the box, then lifted the cover. She frowned in puzzlement as she took out something wrapped in tissue paper. She unfolded that to reveal a small porcelain figurine of a cat sitting on its haunches, and wearing an enigmatic expression.

"It looks exactly like my Ulysses," she said with obvious delight. "Oh, thank you, James. I'll treasure it."

She showed the figurine to Kyle, who rolled his eyes and muttered something that sounded like, "Not another cat!" James could tell the saloon keeper was thinking of his own gift to his bride-to-be.

Once everyone had settled down, Kyle rose and addressed the room, his commanding presence silencing all. "As you all know, Abby has done me the great honor of consenting to become my wife. And I don't have to tell anyone what I've got right here in my shirt pocket."

Jace said, "You surely don't, Kyle."

Everyone else smiled politely.

Kyle fished out the ring, and reached for Abby's hand. She stared up at him, love shining from her eyes.

Kyle grinned like a man who'd just struck pay dirt. "This ring makes it official."

James looked away so he wouldn't see Kyle slip the ring on Abby's finger. When he heard murmurs of congratulations and best wishes for happiness, he looked back to see Abby standing by her fiancé's side, holding his hand.

Maddy rose. "I guess I'll have to go take a look at that ring."

James joined her, though his heart wasn't in it.

Later that night, Abby sat up in bed and moved her left hand this way and that so that the small diamond would catch the lamplight and sparkle.

She smiled and hugged her knees to keep from floating up to the ceiling. Now she experienced firsthand what it meant to walk on air.

Her smile faded. She wished her family could share her happiness unconditionally, but she'd sensed a reserve descend like a cloud on the parlor after Kyle had given her the ring. They all still had their doubts about him.

Their doubts had even affected James. He'd come up to her, given her a peck on the cheek, and offered his best wishes for her future happiness, then shook hands with Kyle. But his dark eyes looked remote and troubled.

Abby extinguished her lamp and slid under the covers. Her family had nothing to worry about. Kyle had promised her that once he owned One-Eyed Jack's he would make sweeping changes, and the girls would go. Her family would see that he was a man of integrity. They'd admit they were wrong about him.

She closed her eyes and slept.

In her dream, she was back in Chicago, walking to school. She saw Kyle walking down the street with one of the men who'd abducted her. She stopped, bewildered. Before she could ask her beloved fiancé what he was doing in the company of such a thug, Kyle and his partner grabbed her and forced her into a waiting carriage painted a gleaming gold.

She struggled.

"Kyle!" she screamed. "What are you doing?"

He said nothing, just gagged her while his partner bound her wrists. Then they sat across from her. Kyle still wouldn't speak.

Magically, the ropes loosened and fell away. She pulled off her gag and flung open the carriage door. Clawing hands reached for her as she jumped down into the street.

She tried to run, but her feet had turned to stone, so heavy to lift, so disobedient. Every step was such an effort, she felt as though she were running through a sticky sea of glue.

Then Kyle caught her, his fingers digging into her shoulders so painfully she screamed.

And screamed.

"Abby, honey, wake up."

Her eyes flew open. She found herself in her own bed, her mother sitting beside her, a comforting hand on her shoulder.

"You had a bad dream," her mother said, her pale eyes soft and worried.

Lizzie stood nearby, holding a lamp. "More like a full-blown nightmare."

Abby sat up, took a deep, shuddering breath, and let it out. Cold, acrid sweat drenched her nightgown. Her heart raced. "I dreamed that I was being abducted."

By Kyle.

"Your screaming woke us," Lizzie said. "You sounded like you were being skinned alive."

"I'm fine now," Abby said with a wan smile. "It was only a bad dream. Sorry to wake you. Go back to bed."

"You sure you're all right?" her mother said. "Would you like a cup of hot milk? Do you want Lizzie to stay with you? Shall we leave the lamp on?"

"That's not necessary. I'll be fine."

Her mother kissed Abby on the forehead, then she and Lizzie left.

Through the door, Abby heard James say, "Is everything all right? I heard Abby scream."

"She had a nightmare," her mother replied, "but she's fine now."

When Abby heard their bedroom doors close, she rose and changed her nightgown. She didn't return to bed. She crossed the room to the rocking chair by the window and sat quietly in the darkness.

She still hadn't fully recovered from the effects of the dream. Traces of the fear and panic lingered, imprinting the vivid dream on her mind so that she remembered every horrible detail.

Why had she dreamed that Kyle was one of her abductors?

She twisted her engagement ring. They loved each other. He would never do such a thing to her.

Her only explanation was that she'd been thinking of

Kyle so much lately, her thoughts about him had somehow gotten all jumbled up with the abduction in her
mind, resulting in the dream.

She was glad she'd had the presence of mind not to
tell her mother and Lizzie.

"It was only a dream," she said aloud. "It doesn't
mean anything."

She rose and returned to bed.

She'd have to tell Kyle. Her dream would certainly
give him a good chuckle.

"I heard you scream last night," James said.

Abby, riding beside him on their way to Jace's, pulled
absently at Fireworks's mane. "I had another nightmare
about being abducted."

"That's what your mother told me when I went out
into the hall to see what was wrong." He looked at her,
his gaze soft and sympathetic. "They'll stop eventually."

She shuddered, vestiges of the dream still lingering
like the sour smell of smoke after a fire. "Can we please
talk about something else?"

James rode his blood bay mare in silence for several
minutes. He looked around at bare fields where the snow
had begun to melt during this mild winter, leaving dry
brown patches.

"I'm going to miss this place," he said.

They were leaving for Chicago tomorrow.

"You can always come back for a visit during spring
break, or in the summer," Abby said. "Kyle and I will
be married, but my folks would be happy to put you
up."

He stared out into the distance, his expression remote

and unreadable. "I'm sure I'll be busy with my own practice."

Abby realized that this reticent, private man had never discussed his plans after graduation, and she'd been so preoccupied with her own that she'd never asked.

"Where do you want to practice?" she said.

"Ever since I decided to become a vet, I've dreamed of finding a small town somewhere, hanging out my shingle, and buying a farm. Maybe in Illinois, or Iowa, or farther out West. I haven't decided."

"With Dr. Kendall retiring, Little Falls might have enough work for two vets. You could open a practice here."

"No."

Abby looked at him, surprised by his flat rejection of the possibility. "Why not? You just said that you dreamed of opening a practice in a small town, and buying a farm. You said you were going to miss this place."

"If Kyle plans to buy Jack's, and you plan to raise a family, you'll need all the work you can get," he said. "You don't need any competition from me."

Abby patted her mare's arched neck. "You're right." The sooner Kyle bought the saloon and dismissed the girls, the sooner he'd put her family's misgivings to rest.

"Besides," he said, "I'll always have that beautiful picture Lizzie painted for me as a memento of my Christmas in Little Falls."

Abby envisioned James sitting alone in his office somewhere, with the watercolor hanging on the wall, and she felt irrational tears sting her eyes. She fought them back. She was being silly and sentimental.

"Shall we let the horses run the rest of the way?" James said. "Mine's about ready to jump out of her skin."

Abby nodded and touched her heels to Fireworks.

They cantered together, the horses moving at the same leisurely speed, matching strides. Abby couldn't help glancing over at James, for he hadn't been exaggerating when he said he was an expert rider.

He caught her staring. "What are you looking at?" he asked over the thunder of hoofbeats.

"Your seat," she replied.

When he grinned, she added hastily, "In the saddle. Your seat in the saddle."

"That's what I thought."

In a few minutes, they arrived at Abby's grandfather's farm and cantered down the long drive, past the familiar wood-frame house. The place hadn't been the same since Grandmama Clementine's death. Then Jace's long-time housekeeper and her husband had retired to their own little spread some miles away, leaving Jace at the mercy of the dour Swedish woman he'd hired to cook and clean.

No sooner did Abby and James ride into the stable yard and dismount than Jace approached them. One look at her grandfather's grim expression told Abby that something was amiss.

"Just the folks I want to see. Two of my stallions just got into a fight. Sycamore got torn up pretty bad."

"Any severed veins or arteries?" Abby asked. "Any broken bones?"

"No, thank God," Jace replied.

Abby looked over at James. "Let's go patch him up."

Jace led the way into the barn, where the battered chestnut stallion named Sycamore stood quiet and sub-dued in a box stall because one of the grooms had ap-plied a twitch to the horse's sensitive upper lip and was holding him.

"I suppose you think we shouldn't use a twitch," Abby said to James, referring to an old disagreement.

He gave her a wry look. "I think it's necessary in this case."

Sycamore's hindquarters, chest, and neck had several open cuts from where his adversary had kicked and bitten him.

"I've already cleaned the wounds," Jace said, rubbing his jaw. "I was just about to suture them myself, but sometimes my hand shakes."

Abby looked at James. "We'll do it."

"Where are your pins and suture wires?" James asked.

Jace indicated a box of medical supplies on the floor. "Right here."

Once they took off their coats, rolled up their sleeves, and washed their hands, James said to Abby, "You take the left side, and I'll take the right."

Abby was relieved to see that the wounds were still fresh enough to suture, so they'd heal quickly if the two cut edges were brought together.

Most of the wounds on the stallion's left side were so minor Abby could unite the cuts' divided edges with a single pin and a simple close-hitch suture. Only one gash on the hindquarters was long and deep enough to require five pins, weaving the sutures from each pin's head to point in a figure-eight pattern.

"Easy boy," she murmured soothingly before inserting each pin. "This is only going to sting a little bit."

Sycamore snorted noisily, but didn't move a muscle, the threat of the twitch keeping him still.

"When we're through with you, you'll still be a handsome devil," James said, causing the stallion to cock one ear back at the sound of his voice. "Abby's sutures are so fine, they barely leave a scar."

She smiled at his compliment. "Yours aren't bad, either, Bradshaw, for someone who isn't valedictorian."

"Senior year's not over yet, Cooper," he retorted.

When they were finished, Jace inspected their handiwork and nodded in approval.

"You two make a pretty good team," he said. "Ever think of going into business together?"

James avoided Abby's gaze as he rolled down his sleeves. "Hadn't even crossed our minds."

Kyle stood in front of One-Eyed Jack's and waved as the buggy carrying Abby and Bradshaw off to the train station rolled down Main Street.

She'd be back in Chicago, and he'd be free until April. Spring break, she called it. The next time she'd come home.

Three months to do as he pleased.

He smiled as he went back inside.

Once in his office, he sat down at his desk and took out the ledger bound in fine maroon calfskin that Abby's parents had given him for Christmas. Was that the best they could come up with, a damn ledger? He could buy a cheaper one himself at the mercantile, and it'd do the job.

He'd been hoping they'd give him money, a little something to put toward buying Jack's. After all, he'd just gotten engaged to their daughter. You'd think they'd want to set up their future son-in-law in business. Hell, they could afford it. And more.

"Is she gone?" came a sultry, hopeful voice from the doorway.

He turned in his swivel chair to see Minnie standing

there, her brown eyes shining with promise, an expectant smile on her full, rosy lips.

"Until April," he replied.

She smiled and glided over, her rounded hips swaying provocatively, her low-cut bodice exposing an expanse of plump, jiggling white bosom. "While the cat's away . . ."

Kyle grinned and reached for her. "The mice will play."

14

Abby glanced around the campus, looking for any sign of Rockwell Shays.

Since she and James had returned to Chicago, she'd fought hard to keep her memories of Little Falls fresh in her mind. Oh, she couldn't wait to see Ulysses, who caught a mouse in the cellar and proudly dropped it at her feet as a welcome-home offering. She greeted Josie with a hug, who responded by plying both her boarders with enough food to feed an army, while she drank in every bit of news about everybody, and told about her own visit to her sister in Evanston. But after this last return to Little Falls, Abby found she missed her home and family more than ever.

Sometimes she slipped into James's bedroom so she could look at Lizzie's watercolor that he'd hung above his desk, and imagine that she was back in Missouri, mounted on her horse and gazing out contentedly over those same green fields.

Maybe it was because she and Kyle were officially engaged, and she was impatient to marry him and begin their future together. At first, she refused to wear gloves, even on a cold day like this one, just in case she wanted to look at his ring for the millionth time. She put them back on when an angry and appalled James pointed out that by the time they arrived at the college, her hands would be too stiff to take a culture or suture a wound.

Now, as she and James crossed the quadrangle, she mentally forced herself to return to the reality of making her other dream come true.

"Do you realize that we haven't seen Shays since we got back?" Abby said.

"I'm sure he's here somewhere. Skulking in doorways. Hiding under a rock."

Abby looked around. Still no sign of Shays or his cronies. "Since Sergeant O'Reilly hasn't come calling, I think it's safe to assume the police no longer suspect us of being a party to Shays's beating."

"I'm sure they've gone on to more serious crimes, and more dangerous lawbreakers."

"Haven't you ever wondered who *did* beat him?"

"It was obviously somebody who's seen Shays harassing you, and wanted to put a stop to it." He smiled. "Maybe one of our fellow students is a secret admirer."

Abby stared at him in astonishment. "I can't believe that. Most of my male classmates would just as soon see me fail."

"Maybe Piggy Hogg hired some thug."

Abby's jaw dropped, then she burst out laughing. "Dr. Hogg hire a thug to beat up a student? I've never heard of anything so—so ludicrous. He's a college professor. A man of high intellect and moral principles. He wouldn't know the first thing about hiring a thug."

A smile tugged at the corners of James's mouth. "Well, perhaps that was a bit farfetched." His smile died. "If that beating keeps Shays from bothering you,

I'd say they ought to give whoever did it a medal."

Abby looked at him in surprise. "I don't approve of violence, even if I ultimately benefit."

"Usually neither do I. But I've also learned that sometimes violence is the only language a bully understands."

She wondered what had happened in his life to make him draw that conclusion. She was just about to satisfy her curiosity by asking him when his expression turned remote.

"Maybe the beating won't stop Shays," she said.

"Then I would imagine he risks the culprit doing it again."

When they arrived in class, they took their seats in the last row. Other students entered and sat down at their desks. Still no sign of Shays or his cronies.

Abby glanced at the wall clock. One minute to go before the professor arrived and called the class to order. Still no Shays.

She drummed her fingers against the desktop. She opened her notebook, then closed it. She listened as footsteps approached the door.

The door opened.

Shays, Evans, and Hendries walked in.

Abby stared at Shays. His bruises had disappeared. He looked none the worse for wear.

She braced herself.

Shays glared daggers at her but said nothing. He and his friends walked to the head of the class and took their seats.

Abby let out the breath she'd been holding. Did she dare hope this was the end of Shays's campaign to force her out of school? She looked over at James.

He leaned forward and whispered so only she could

hear. "I guess Shays got your anonymous champion's message."

She shook her head sadly. She didn't want an anonymous champion beating and injuring someone on her behalf. "The end hardly justifies the means."

"At least now he'll stop bothering you."

Later that afternoon after classes were over for the day, Abby went back to the boardinghouse alone, and James stayed to do some research in the library.

When he finished at five o'clock, he packed up his books and notes and left. No sooner did he step out of the library than a familiar black-coated figure materialized at his side.

"Jimmy," Parson Brown said in his flat rasp. "Haven't seen you around in a while."

White-hot fury sent the blood rushing to James's face. He didn't look at the Parson, and he didn't stop walking. "What in the hell are you doing here?" he snapped, quickening his stride, casting darting glances at the few students who passed, praying he didn't recognize any of his classmates, and that Shays and his friends weren't around.

"We have to talk," the Parson said, matching his stride to James's.

"You beat up a student, then you dare show your face on this campus." He shook with rage. "Are you out of your mind, or just stupid?"

If being called stupid offended the Parson, he didn't show it. "Just following orders," was his calm reply.

"If Shays or one of his friends sees us talking together and gets suspicious, the police will come sniffing around again. That's a complication I don't want or need."

"Don't worry. The alley was dark, and I made sure Shays wouldn't recognize me."

James risked a furious glance at Nick's henchman. "Get out of here and leave me alone."

"I can't do that until we've talked."

"No."

"There's this bar near here."

"Even if no one can identify you, I won't risk being seen with you. Do I make myself clear?"

"I've got the boss's carriage. Why don't I drive around the block and meet you at the corner? Nobody'll be the wiser."

"No."

The Parson shrugged. "I got my orders, Jimmy. If you won't talk to me in the carriage, then I'll just follow you back to that boardinghouse of yours and present myself at the front door."

He could just see the expression on Abby's face when the shady-looking character she'd seen James talking to in Kachinsky's alley suddenly showed up at the front door. He could just hear the suspicion in her voice when she started asking the inevitable questions.

One look at the Parson, and she'd surely suspect James of involvement in Shays's beating.

"Ride around the block, and I'll meet you at the corner."

The Parson's mouth stretched into a grim parody of a smile. "I knew you'd listen to reason."

"More like blackmail," James retorted, fighting to control his temper.

Five minutes later, Nick's carriage stopped at the corner and the door opened. James resisted the impulse to look around to make sure he wasn't being observed because he knew that would only call attention to himself.

Instead he climbed inside the carriage as if he were accepting a ride from a friend. He'd learned a thing or two from Nick.

He sat across from the Parson and glared at him. "You just jeopardized everything I've worked for."

The Parson's cold, soulless eyes registered no emotion. "Relax. It's late. Classes are over for the day. Nobody's around to see us together. I made sure of that before I approached you."

James knew he spoke the truth. If anything, Nick's man was a consummate professional.

"Which cop is bothering you?" the Parson asked.

"Why do you want to know? Will Nick have you beat him up, too?"

"I don't beat up cops. Just thought that he might be on Nick's payroll."

"Is there anybody Nick can't buy?"

"Every man has his price, Jimmy. Even you."

James gritted his teeth. "I don't want any more favors from Nick. He's done too much as it is."

"He's your father. He's concerned about you."

"What do you want to talk to me about? Make it quick. I've got studying to do."

The Parson unbuttoned his top coat button. "Nick wants to know why you didn't come for Christmas. He was looking forward to it, and he was disappointed when you didn't show up."

"I went away for the holiday," James replied.

"I gathered that when I went by the boardinghouse and saw that it was all dark and deserted. You should tell Mrs. Wachowski to have somebody look after her house while she's gone. You know, leave a light on at night so the building looks like there's somebody there.

Otherwise she's going to come home someday and find nothing left but the light fixtures."

James thought of Parson Brown moving noiselessly through Josie's house, opening desk drawers, rifling through private papers, violating their privacy. He almost went for the Parson's throat, then fought down the impulse. "You didn't."

"No."

But he could have. James knew that all too well.

"Nick wants to know where you went," the Parson said.

"None of his business."

The other man sighed. "Nick told me to find out, and I will. If you don't tell me, I'll have to get the information some other way. Like ask Mrs. Wachowski, or that pretty little Miss Cooper."

James sat back against the cushion. He couldn't risk having Parson Brown anywhere near Josie or Abby.

"Miss Cooper invited me to spend Christmas with her and her family in Missouri," he said.

Surprise momentarily illuminated the Parson's expressionless features. "Must be serious, if she took you home to meet her family."

"Get it through your thick skull that Miss Cooper and I are just friends. She invited me to go home with her because I had nowhere else to go, and she felt sorry for me."

"You could've spent Christmas with Nick."

"I'd rather eat nails."

Brown actually laughed, a wheezing chuckle like a death rattle. "Eat nails . . . that's funny." When he stopped, he said, "Nick'll want to know if you had a good time. What'll I tell him?"

"Tell him I had a very good time."

Except when Abby accepted Lambert's ring.

"I would've thought a city boy like you would go crazy in the country with all those cows and sheep. All that quiet."

"I found it a pleasant change from all the noise and bustle of Chicago."

The Parson studied him. "This Shays fellow. He's been leaving Miss Cooper alone?"

"So far," James grudgingly admitted.

"I'm not surprised." A rare, full-blown smile warmed the Parson's face. "He was real easy to convince."

Several days later, after Abby finished assisting Dr. Emerson with a difficult and complicated abdominal surgery on a horse, she cleaned up while James waited. They left together. Just as James reached the front door, he stopped in his tracks.

"I forgot to ask Emerson something. You go on ahead. I'll catch up."

"Are you sure? I can wait." Actually, she'd put in a long night studying, and she wanted nothing more than a hot soak in the bathtub, and a nap.

"No, you go ahead."

Abby left the building and started across campus. When she reached the street, she noticed an automobile parked by the curb. The vehicle caught her attention because among the usual horse-drawn carriages, the automobile appeared as out of place as an elephant in a parlor.

Abby smiled to herself. She could just imagine the ruckus an automobile would cause in Little Falls if it came speeding down Main Street. Dogs would bark. Horses would bolt. The quilting circle would be struck dumb.

She herself had been startled when she first arrived in Chicago and one drove by the boardinghouse, brazenly honking its horn for Mr. Kachinsky's meat wagon to get out of its way. After the shock wore off, she'd been fascinated. Imagine riding in a conveyance that didn't depend on a horse.

Abby longed to ride in one. Regina had, during a visit to St. Louis. She said her heart was in her mouth when the ride started, but once they'd gone a few miles, she found it exhilarating.

As Abby approached the automobile, which was running, the driver got out and walked around the front.

He was none other than the man she'd seen James talking to in the alley.

And he was walking toward her.

"Miss Cooper," he said.

If Abby hadn't been so tired, perhaps she would have remembered Josie's lessons about steering clear of strange men. But she wasn't thinking clearly. She stopped when he said her name.

The man would have looked menacing enough in his black hat and long black coat that appeared large and loose enough to conceal another man within its folds. But when Abby looked into his rain gray eyes and saw nothing there, she felt a sharp jolt of fear.

"Miss Cooper," he said, opening the automobile's door, "my name is Brown. Will you please come with me."

The men who'd abducted her hadn't asked politely. They'd just shoved her into the waiting carriage. Bound and gagged her. Took her to that dark, deserted building and frightened her half to death.

She looked around as she took one step back, then

another. This part of the street was deserted. No one would help her if she screamed.

"I don't care who you are. I'm not going anywhere with you."

She also didn't care if he and James were friends. There was something unsavory about him. Something cold and heartless.

"I'm not going to hurt you," he said.

She didn't believe him. Abby turned to flee. She didn't take more than three strides when Brown grabbed her arm and said something that stopped her cold.

"If you care about your landlady, you'll come with me."

Josie.

Abby turned and hugged her books to keep her arms from shaking. "What have you done with her?"

"Nothing."

"Then why are you threatening me?"

Annoyance flitted across his melancholy features. "You've seen me talking with James Bradshaw. Would a friend of his hurt you?"

"He wouldn't allow it."

"Then get in."

James strode out of the building, eager to catch up to Abby. He'd spent far too much time with the long-winded Dr. Emerson. Abby was probably halfway home by now.

She wasn't.

He saw her talking to Parson Brown, who was holding open the passenger side to Nick's parked automobile. Then Abby climbed inside and Brown shut the door.

James shouted her name.

He dropped his books and ran.

But he wasn't fast enough.

The automobile pulled away, cutting too close in front of a skittish horse pulling a buggy. The animal screamed and reared. One driver cursed the other. The automobile rolled down the street, picking up speed, oblivious to the commotion it was causing in its wake. Finally it took a turn and disappeared down a side street.

James kept running until a stitch stabbed at his side and his breath was coming in shallow gasps. Pedestrians turned to stare.

What had the Parson said to make her go willingly?

"God *damn* him!"

He hurried down the street to find a cab or a streetcar. Brown would arrive at Nick's long before James did. He hoped his father used the time to pray, because if he dared hurt Abby, this time James would kill him.

Abby was too scared to enjoy her first automobile ride.

She sat rigid in her soft, luxurious leather seat, her arms pressed stiff against her sides, her books in her lap. She stared straight ahead, but kept watching Brown out of the corner of her eye.

"Where are you taking me?" Her voice sounded thin and reedy. Frightened.

"To meet Nick Flynn."

"I don't know any Nick Flynn."

"He knows you."

Stay calm and don't panic, Abby told herself. *He knows James, and he said he wasn't going to hurt you.*

She forced herself to concentrate on the ride. The automobile rode more smoothly than a carriage, and faster, but it was odd not to see a horse up front, its head bobbing, and hear the steady clop-clop-clop of iron-shod hooves on pavement. Instead she heard the flat mechanical hum of the engine.

Brown appeared skilled in handling the machine. He wove down the street and didn't hit any pedestrians or horses, though he did have several close calls that caused Abby to screw her eyes shut, hold her breath, and pray.

Her reaction amused Brown. "You look green around the gills. Ever ride in one of these before?"

"First time," Abby choked out. "Do they always go this fast?"

"Fast? This is crawling. You should see it on a country road. I can get it up to forty miles per hour."

"You must feel like you're flying."

He chuckled, then fell silent.

Abby lost all track of time and sense of direction. She felt as though she'd been riding with Brown for hours. She took careful note of her surroundings, looking for anything familiar, trying to memorize the names of unknown streets and buildings. Much to her relief, she saw not one deserted warehouse or rundown factory. Her spirits lifted a fraction when she realized they were driving through the Loop, the city's crowded business district.

If he meant to harm her, he'd surely take her somewhere less populated.

But his threat against Josie still hung between them.

Abby sat back and resisted the impulse to open the door and make a run for it. Surely she'd be able to find a policeman or someone to protect her.

James.

What had he thought when he finished talking to Dr. Emerson and tried to catch up with her? Did he wonder what had happened, or did he assume she'd beat him back to the boardinghouse? Surely he'd arrived there by now. What would he think when he looked at the rack in the hall and didn't see her coat and scarf hanging there?

She looked at Brown. "James will be worried when he returns to the boardinghouse and sees I'm not there."

"He'll stop worrying when I bring you back safe and sound."

Fifteen minutes later, the automobile stopped.

"We're here," Brown said.

She looked out the window and saw that they were parked in front of a stone mansion. She was more relieved than surprised. The minute the automobile had turned onto Lake Shore Drive and she saw Lake Michigan, she knew Brown had driven her to an exclusive part of the city.

Surely she couldn't be in danger here.

A man appeared and walked with feline grace down the steps leading up to the mansion.

"The boss himself," Brown said. "You should feel honored. His guests usually go to *him*."

Butterflies fluttered in the pit of Abby's stomach. Now she would meet the mysterious Nick Flynn and learn why he'd sent his man to bring her here.

Abby watched the tall, well-dressed man approach. Distinguished and good looking, he had wings of silver sweeping from his temples through black hair.

Why did Abby have the uneasy feeling that she'd met him somewhere? If she had, surely she would remember such a distinctive gentleman.

He opened the door and extended his hand to help her alight. "Miss Cooper, what a pleasure to meet you," he said in a deep, cultured voice. "I'm Nick Flynn."

Abby ignored his outstretched hand and disembarked from the automobile with as much aplomb as she could muster. She hugged her books, using them as a physical barrier while she faced Nick Flynn.

"I can't say that the pleasure is all mine, sir," she said coldly. "I resent being kidnapped."

"Kidnapped?" Amusement tugged at the corners of his mouth and warmed his cool blue eyes. "I merely invited you to meet me."

"Your invitation was rather forceful."

He smiled. "I have been told that I possess a rather forceful personality."

Abby raised her chin. "So have I."

Nick Flynn burst out laughing. "I've always admired a woman with spirit. Please. Come inside. We have much to discuss."

Abby wondered what she could possible have to discuss with Nick Flynn.

15

❧

NICK FLYNN LIVED IN A FORTRESS.

Abby couldn't understand why a man would feel compelled to surround himself with thick stone walls. To keep someone out? Or someone in?

While Flynn spoke with his butler, Abby stood stiffly in the center of the round stone foyer, looking for escape routes and hugging her books to hide her anxiety. She inspected a dark, medieval-looking tapestry hanging on the opposite wall. She'd never been inside a castle, but she imagined this mansion closely duplicated one.

This Flynn was obviously a wealthy man living in luxury. Why would he risk it all by kidnapping a woman? She didn't even know him.

A low "woof" interrupted her reflection. She turned to see a huge mastiff standing in an arched doorway.

"Is he friendly?" she said to Flynn.

"Moriarty can be *too* friendly," he replied. "Call him. He'll come to you."

"Come here, boy."

The mastiff walked toward her warily. Abby made a fist and extended her hand so he could learn her scent.

Moriarty sniffed her thoroughly, then licked her hand with one swipe, his tail wagging and his black wrinkled face brightening into a canine grin.

"Good dog," Abby said, petting his broad head at arm's length so he wouldn't slobber on her skirt. She really preferred cats. At least they didn't drool.

Flynn joined her. "He's my son's dog."

She looked at him warily. "Mr. Flynn, why have you brought me here?"

Humor warmed his icy eyes attractively. "I'll explain everything to you all in good time, Miss Cooper."

He extended his hand, indicating that she should precede him through a doorway. She contemplated throwing her books at him and making a run for it, then decided against it. If the dog didn't stop her before she reached the front door, the butler or the man who had brought her here surely would.

Best to play along and wait for the right opportunity.

The first thing Abby noticed when she found herself in another, larger hallway was the commanding portrait. The second thought that crossed her mind was the feeling she'd seen this woman somewhere before.

But that was impossible. She'd only just met Flynn. She certainly didn't know anyone in his family.

She stopped and stared. "Your wife?"

"The love of my life."

"She's very beautiful."

"Was. My Lucy died five years ago."

"I'm sorry."

"Don't be. The time we did have together was a most wonderful gift."

Abby thought of her own parents and the enduring love they shared. "That's all any of us can hope for."

He inclined his head slightly, ushered her down another hallway, and stopped before a pair of doors. "My study," he said as he opened them and stood back so Abby could enter.

She felt even more out of place once she stepped inside the elegant room, for she was more comfortable in simple, utilitarian surroundings. Yet she appreciated the sensuous luxury of smelling sweet hothouse flowers in the middle of winter, and the elegance of sitting on a soft leather sofa.

"I've taken the liberty of ordering tea," Flynn said, pulling on an embroidered bell pull. "Unless, of course, you'd prefer something stronger. Champagne, perhaps?"

Abby enjoyed an occasional brandy with Kyle or her father, but she had never tasted champagne, and she almost succumbed to the temptation to try something new. However she suspected she was going to need her wits about her to deal with this man, so she declined his offer.

Her gaze fell on the weapons displayed on the far wall, behind Flynn's large pedimented desk.

She rose and walked over to look at the swords, daggers, and pistols. "These seem rather out of place in such an elegant, beautiful room."

"Do you think so?" He walked over to stand beside her. "I like to think of them as a reminder that in this world, violence exists side by side with beauty."

Abby shivered, her wariness increasing. She faced him squarely. "Mr. Flynn, I've got studying to do, and I have to get back to the boardinghouse. If you're not going to tell me why you had me brought here, I—"

A knock at the door interrupted her. "That should be Gardiner, with tea," Flynn said. "Excuse me."

He crossed the room and opened the door to admit the butler pushing a tea cart laden with a gleaming silver service, delicate china cups, and an assortment of dainty pastel frosted cakes the likes of which even a good cook like Josie could never hope to duplicate.

"Take tea with me, Miss Cooper," Flynn said with a charming, persuasive smile. "Then I'll tell you why I invited you here."

Abby could see that she'd only be wasting time arguing. "Very well."

She sat down on the sofa and set her books down beside her while Flynn dismissed his butler and proceeded to serve her himself. When Abby had her cup and a small plate of cakes, Flynn poured tea for himself and sat down across from her on the matching sofa.

"The cakes are my chef's specialty," he told her. "I hope you like them."

She sampled one. "Delicious."

Flynn smiled. "He'll be delighted to hear you thought so."

Though seething with impatience, Abby forced herself to remain calm, politely answering Flynn's questions about school and what she thought of Chicago.

When she finished her tea, she set down the cup with a determined clink. She rose. "All right, Mr. Flynn, the time for polite conversation is over. If you're not going to tell me why you brought me here—"

"I brought you here," he said, dabbing his lips fastidiously with a napkin, "to discuss your relationship with my son."

James brushed past the butler at the door and strode into the foyer. "Where in the hell is she?"

"In the study, Mr. James," Gardiner said, "but your father gave express orders that they are not to be disturbed. By anyone."

James ignored him and kept on walking. Gardiner knew better than to try to stop him.

When Moriarty appeared, his tail wagging and an expectant doggy smile on his face, James snapped, ''Lie down!''

The mastiff whined and his head drooped as he slunk off to a nearby corner. He lay down and rested on his head on his forelegs, his soulful brown eyes regarding James in abject misery.

James had to find Abby.

Abby stared incredulously at Flynn. ''I don't have a relationship with your son. I don't even know anyone named Flynn.''

Without warning, the study's double doors suddenly flew open and crashed against the walls, causing Abby to start and turn in her seat.

Flynn rose.

James stood poised in the doorway, his face contorted into a dark mask of rage, his eyes glowing like hot coals.

Before Abby could even ask him what he was doing here, James strode over to Flynn, and in the blink of an eye, drew back his arm and hit the older man in the jaw with such force that he staggered back.

''James!'' Abby cried, appalled, rising.

Flynn crashed into the tea cart and went down with it like a felled oak. Silver and china went clinking and clattering to the floor, sending a spray of tea and hot water into the air. Cakes disappeared, squashed.

Though she hardly recognized the violent man standing there, Abby hurried to James's side and laid a hand on his arm. He stared at her out of dark, unseeing eyes, his nostrils flaring with every panting breath.

Then his rage abruptly died.

"Are you all right?" he demanded, framing her face with his hands and regarding her with such burning intensity that Abby thought she'd ignite. "He didn't hurt you?"

"We were having tea." When James closed his eyes and sighed shakily, she said, "Am I glad to see you. Now, would you mind explaining what is going on?"

Flynn hauled himself to his feet and stood there swaying unsteadily. The blow had disheveled his hair, and the fall spattered his suit with dark tea stains. Blood trickled from one corner of his mouth, but a curious light of triumph burned in his eyes.

James's hands fell away from Abby's cheeks, and he placed himself between her and Flynn, physically protecting her with his own body as he had during the snowball fight with Shays.

A low, warning growl coming from the doorway momentarily distracted them, and they all looked to see Gardiner standing there, restraining the mastiff by his thick leather collar. Then the dog whined in confusion, not knowing which of his masters was the attacker, and which had been attacked.

"I heard a commotion, sir," the butler said, "and came to investigate."

Flynn waved him away. "We're fine. Take the dog and close the doors behind you."

The butler kept one hand on the mastiff's collar while he closed one door, then the other. His footsteps sounded down the hall, then silence enveloped the study.

Flynn took a handkerchief out of his breast pocket and dabbed at his bleeding mouth. He looked at Abby. "I see he hasn't told you."

Abby glanced at James, who was regarding Flynn with the rage and desperation of a cornered wild animal.

"Told me what?" she demanded.

"That he's my son," Flynn replied.

"You're lying," she snapped. "His name is Bradshaw, not Flynn. He has no family."

"Abby, it's true," James said in a weary voice. "He is my father."

She felt suspiciously like Lewis Carroll's Alice who had just fallen down the rabbit hole to find herself wandering amidst strange creatures. She looked from James to Flynn and back to James.

In a heartbeat, she realized why she'd thought she'd met Flynn somewhere before. While the resemblance wasn't exact, the men shared enough of one to be father and son.

Looking at James's bleak, tormented expression, Abby realized she had to get him away from Nick Flynn and back to the boardinghouse. The dozens of questions breeding like rabbits in her mind would have to go unanswered for a little while.

"James," she said firmly, retrieving her books, "I want to leave. Let's go home."

"But we haven't even begun to get acquainted," Flynn said. "Stay for dinner. My chef—"

"We are leaving," Abby said in a sharp, imperious tone that would have put Regina to shame. "I think that under the circumstances, you can provide the transportation."

Flynn studied her out of narrowed eyes for what seemed like an eternity. Undaunted, Abby stood her ground and stared right back.

"You heard the lady," James said.

Flynn smiled. "My carriage is at your disposal."

• • • •

Late afternoon light flooded the interior of the luxurious, well-sprung carriage. Abby sat across from James, her books next to her on the seat. After he handed her inside and sat down, he asked her several times if she was all right. She assured him that she was. Then he fell silent, shrouded in his own thoughts as he stared out the window.

Abby said nothing, respecting his need for silence. She hoped her presence soothed him, for she knew this afternoon's events had left both of them shaken.

He turned his head and looked at her. "I owe you an explanation."

"You owe me several," she said gently, "but they can wait until we're back home."

He nodded and turned his attention back to the window.

"Where are your books and notes?" she asked, noticing they weren't with him.

He gave her a blank look. "I must've dropped them when I chased you and the automobile."

Abby made a small sound of dismay. "If whoever finds them doesn't turn them in, you can borrow mine."

"After listening to what I have to say, you may never want to speak to me again."

"Surely it can't be that bad."

His pained look told her that it could.

When they arrived at the boardinghouse, they found only Ulysses seated on the stairs, and a note from Josie telling them that she'd gone to visit her friend next door.

As James helped her with her coat, Abby felt relieved that they would have some privacy.

"I'll pour some root beers," she said, "and we can talk in the parlor."

James rubbed his face. "This is one time I wish Josie

kept something stronger than root beer in the house."

Abby had a feeling that by the time James finished telling his story, she'd be yearning for more than root beer herself.

When she returned to the parlor with their drinks, she found James seated in the Stickley chair, his elbows propped on his knees and his head bowed, the picture of dejection.

She handed him his drink, and sat down across from him.

His dark, brooding gaze held hers. "First, you'll want me to explain why I lied to you and Josie about having no family in Chicago."

"That was my first question," she admitted.

"I'm Nick Flynn's illegitimate son," he said.

"So that's why your surnames are different."

"Yes. He and my mother never married. I kept her name."

"The beautiful woman in the portrait on the landing. She's your mother." When James nodded, Abby said, "Now I know why she looked so familiar. You have her coloring, especially her dark eyes."

James stared into his glass.

"Is that why you didn't want us to know about your father? You're ashamed of your illegitimacy?" Before he could reply, Abby added, "Surely you can't believe that Josie and I would hold the circumstances of your birth against you."

He shook his head. "I know you wouldn't. And it's not that I'm ashamed of my birth. Once I explain the circumstances to you, you'll understand." He took a deep breath. "I didn't want you to know about my father because *I'm* ashamed of *him*."

"Why? He seems like a fine man. Overbearing, perhaps, and used to getting what he wants. Judging from his home, I'd say he's also quite successful. Surely a father a son could be proud of."

He regarded her with that intensity that always made Abby so uneasy. "Nick Flynn—my father—is a criminal. He's one of the most ruthless vice lords in Chicago."

Abby froze in disbelief, her glass halfway to her lips. She set it down before she spilled her drink.

"You're not making this up," she said.

"I wish I were."

"But he seems so—so cultured. So refined."

James set down his glass and knotted his fingers together. "Yes, it's hard to believe that the urbane, distinguished-looking man in the expensive suits is a ruthless, corrupt killer who—"

"Killer?" Abby's eyes widened. "Oh, James, surely not."

"I'm not exaggerating, Abby. Nick Flynn is as much a killer as those bushwhackers who wiped out Josie's family and shot your grandmother."

She recalled the knives and swords and pistols on Flynn's study walls and she shuddered. What had he said to her? "I like to think of them as a reminder that in this world, violence exists side by side with beauty." He'd also been describing himself.

"Why hasn't he been arrested for his crimes and thrown into jail?" she asked.

"Because he's very clever. He doesn't leave evidence that can connect him to any crime. He also bribes the police, and has a string of lawyers as long as your arm to get him off the hook legally." He shrugged. "Most of the time he has Parson Brown do his dirty work for him."

A chill suddenly swept through Abby like a late autumn frost. "Mr. Brown, the man who took me to him in the automobile?"

James nodded.

"Is he called Parson because he used to be a minister?"

James sat back in his chair, suppressed a smile, and gave Abby an indulgent look. "That's what anyone would assume, but no. I've been told he's called the Parson because years ago, he acquired the reputation of always asking his victims if they wanted a moment to pray before he killed them."

Abby felt the blood drain from her face, leaving her light-headed. She looked helplessly at James. "I was alone in an automobile with a ruthless killer? I think I'm going to faint."

In an instant he left his chair to sit beside her. He placed his hand on the back of her neck and gently brought her head down to her knees.

The dizziness and nausea passed, but his warm fingers still lingered lightly on the back of her neck. "Thank you," she said, raising her head and dislodging his hand. She sat up.

"Poor Abby," he said. "I'll bet you never imagined men like the Parson and Nick existed."

"I may've been brought up on a farm, but I'm hardly a country bumpkin," she retorted. "I know there are evil men in the world. Two of them abducted me, remember?"

"All too well." He rose and slowly walked back and forth. "Nick's not only a killer. He used to own and operate several brothels in the Levee until the crackdown on vice several years ago."

"When I first came to Chicago," Abby said, "and

got off the train, a man came up to me and offered me work.''

''A cadet seeking recruits for a brothel,'' James said. ''He could've been one of many working for Nick.''

Abby studied him thoughtfully. ''James, if you were brought up in such a violent, immoral world, how did you escape becoming a criminal yourself?''

He returned to his seat. ''I have my mother to thank for that.'' He smiled. ''I know what you're thinking. You're wondering how such a beautiful woman got involved with a criminal, bore him a child, and stayed with him.''

''I don't mean to pry.''

''No, I want to tell you about my mother.''

Sensing tension, Ulysses came trotting into the parlor and jumped into Abby's lap. She petted him, finding the movement soothing, even as she gave James her undivided attention.

''My mother was a famous actress,'' he began, ''named Lucille Bradshaw. She was beautiful and talented, the toast of New York City, and only twenty-four years old when she met Nick Flynn.

''Nick was very clever. He made sure she fell in love with him before he revealed the kind of man he really was. By then, she was pregnant.''

Abby felt a sudden surge of sympathy for the young Lucille Bradshaw. ''She was trapped. She loved him too much to leave him, even for her child's sake.''

''Yes, but my mother was determined to have both Nick and her son on her own terms. And in her own way, she was just as clever.''

''What did she do?''

''She refused to marry Nick. She said that while she loved him and would always live with him, she refused to give me my father's name. She thought that if I had a different surname, she'd keep me out of Nick's dangerous world.''

''And did it?''

''Yes.'' His features turned pinched and cold. ''Until today.''

''She must've loved you very much,'' Abby said softly.

''For all her faults, for all her weaknesses, she did. She even made Nick promise never to involve me in his illegal enterprises in any way, or she'd leave him, and he'd never see his son again.''

''And he loved her enough to make such a promise.''

''As much as Nick is capable of loving anyone,'' he said bitterly. ''As soon as I was old enough, my mother sent me to a boarding school in England. I spent my summers with them here in Chicago. Later, as I grew older, I saw less and less of my mother because I spent summers with my English friends on their country estate.''

''That's when you decided that you wanted to become a vet.''

He nodded. ''The estate was as far removed from Nick's world as I could get, and caring for the animals made me feel that I was doing something worthwhile and productive with my life.''

''That's why you've kept to yourself all through college,'' she said.

''I didn't want anyone finding out the identity of my real father, especially someone like Shays. You know what he'd do with that bit of information.''

''Make your life a living hell.'' Abby's eyes widened as a thought suddenly occurred to her. ''The Parson . . . he's the one who beat up Shays, isn't he?''

"He was carrying out Nick's orders. Nick knew you were my friend, and he was offended that someone would dare harass a friend of his son's. That's why the Parson said, 'Leave Miss Cooper alone,' to Shays. It was a warning of the most forceful kind."

Abby raised her brows. "You've known the identity of the culprit all along, and you've never told the police."

His dark gaze bored into hers. "If I did that, I'd only expose my connection to Nick. Not only would I be in danger from my father's enemies, but you and Josie would be as well."

Abby twisted her engagement ring nervously. "That's all we need."

He leaned forward. "When I was just twelve years old, one of my father's rivals tried to assassinate him, my mother, and me. Thanks to my father's bodyguard, we escaped with our lives. True, that was thirteen years ago, but if I came forward about the Parson beating Shays and revealed my connection to Nick, what's to stop one of his rivals from trying to kill me? Or you and Josie?"

Abby hesitated. Part of her found his silence reprehensible, but another part of her understood his need to keep his world and his father's world far, far apart.

"I don't approve of your not telling the police what you know," she said, "but I can understand why." She shivered. "I certainly don't want to become some criminal's target. Or Josie."

"When Sergeant O'Reilly suspected us of being involved," James said, "I also feared that Nick's meddling would jeopardize our careers. Perhaps we'd be expelled or suspended. I couldn't let that happen. Not after we've both worked so hard."

She stroked Ulysses. "Does he often meddle in your life?"

"He promised my mother that he'd always watch out for me, and he's taken that responsibility quite seriously. *Too* seriously. Most of the time, he stays out of my life. But every once in a while . . ." His voice trailed off.

"He sounds a lot like my father. Maybe, for all his faults, he's trying to be the best father he can to you."

James's eyes turned hard and unforgiving. "Nick's not a good father, or a good man. He never has been. He's a ruthless, remorseless killer."

"He's still your father."

James rose and walked over to the window. "Do you know what I fear the most?" Before she could answer, he turned to look at her. "That deep down inside, I'm really just like him."

16

❧❤❧

ABBY DISLODGED HER CAT, ROSE, AND WALKED
over to James.

"You're a kind, decent, caring man, James Bradshaw," she said softly. "I don't think you're anything
like your father."

He looked down at her, his dark eyes unreadable.
"But I have Nick Flynn's blood running through my
veins as well as my mother's, as he takes perverse pleasure in reminding me."

"What do you mean?"

"Didn't you notice him gloating after I hit him?"

"I wondered why he looked so smug when he picked
himself up off the floor."

"That's because I lost my self-control and gave in to
my rage."

"Losing control doesn't make you ruthless, or a
killer." She placed a hind on his arm and drew him back
to his chair. "You're tormenting yourself needlessly."

He sat down and leaned back. "Am I? I wonder."

Abby took her own seat and sat there quietly. She

wished she could do something, say something to ease his torment.

He looked at her. "My mother always wanted me to become a physician. To her, that profession was the height of respectability. After she died, Nick wanted to carry out her wishes, so he made me a proposition. If I agreed to go to medical school and become a doctor, he would give up his white slavery operation."

"He would stop luring young women into prostitution?"

"Yes. His operation was very profitable—one of his best—so he'd be making a great sacrifice. It wasn't an offer he made lightly. He also agreed to pay for my schooling and any expenses by depositing a check in my bank every year on January second."

"You obviously didn't agree to his terms, because you're in veterinary college, not medical school."

"But I did." He paused. "Only I enrolled in veterinary college. When Nick saw what I'd done and demanded an explanation, I told him I had enrolled in a medical school, only a medical school for *animals*. I intended to become a doctor, all right, but an *animal* doctor."

"You tricked him."

"Yes."

"He must've been furious."

"On the contrary. The perverse old bastard was delighted. He just laughed and said I had just proven once again that I was Nick Flynn's son after all." He sighed. "In a way, he was right."

"Did he keep his word about giving up his white slavery operation?"

"Yes, he did."

"So by accepting his offer, you not only gave yourself the opportunity to receive an education to do work you loved, you saved a number of innocent young women from a life of degradation and servitude.''

"Plus I gave Nick a taste of his own medicine," he said dryly, "which pleased me mightily."

"In this case, I think the end justifies the means. And from what I've seen, you're going to make a fine veterinarian." Abby toyed with her engagement ring. "My grandfather Paul—Maddy's husband—wanted to be a veterinarian, but the only schools at the time were in Europe, and his father wouldn't send him abroad. So he went to Harvard and became a physician. Then, when he went out to Little Falls, he finally was able to make his dream of doctoring animals come true."

"You and I are very fortunate," James said, "to be able to have such an opportunity."

"Be grateful for your veterinary schooling no matter how you got it." Abby rose, and James stood as well. "Are you going to tell Josie what you've just told me?"

"No. I think it would upset her unnecessarily." His gaze slid to the floor. "After what happened to her parents, I wouldn't want her to know she's been renting a room to the son of a notorious criminal."

"My grandpapa Jace always said don't rock the boat unless you want to go for a swim," Abby said. She twisted her fingers together. "Will Josie and I be in any danger from your father's enemies now?"

James took her hands. "If I thought that, I'd move out tomorrow and get as far away from the two of you as possible."

Much to her surprise, Abby realized that if he did leave, she'd miss him. "I hope it doesn't come to that." She smiled and squeezed his hands. "Who would I have to walk to school with?"

James returned her smile, and for the first time since they'd returned from Flynn's, the desolation left his eyes.

Sensing he needed comforting, she impulsively slipped her arms around his waist and drew him to her for a chaste hug. Her gesture must have caught him by surprise, for he went rigid. But only for a heartbeat. Then he pressed his cheek to hers and held her tightly.

"Don't worry," she whispered, rubbing his back as she would soothe a child, until she felt the tension leave him. "Everything will be all right."

"I hope so. I wouldn't want anything to happen to you."

Her hands fell away and she stepped back, breaking their embrace. But his hands still lingered at her waist, holding her, connecting them. She stopped and held her breath, waiting for him to release her. He didn't.

Standing so close, she noticed that his eyes weren't fathomless obsidian pools at all, but lit from within by a sudden glimmer of yearning.

She stood transfixed. She couldn't look away.

You shouldn't have hugged him, she heard a little voice say, *because now he's going to kiss you.*

As if he heard the little voice, too, his gaze roved over her face, settling on her lips. Before she could take another breath, he closed his eyes and his mouth came down over hers.

You mustn't.

But I want to.

His lips felt like velvet warmed in front of a fire, light at first, and so intoxicating. She kissed him back, wanting more.

He pulled her closer to him, and she went willingly, savoring the hardness of his lean, muscular body against the yielding softness of hers. They fit together seamlessly as one. Her lips parted of their own volition, and she tasted the spicy sweetness of his mouth.

Her senses sprang to life. She heard the pounding of her own heart, and felt her bones melt. Her skin tingled. A sensual heat tied her insides into knots. And all from just a kiss.

The sound of loud, raised voices outside the parlor window broke the enchantment.

Could it be the Parson? Nick Flynn himself? Abby's eyes flew open in panic, and she pulled away, suddenly disoriented.

James released her and stepped back.

They stared at each other.

Abby looked away and cleared her throat. "That sounded like the Parson."

"No, he'd never be that obvious." But James went to the window and looked out anyway. "Just some men arguing." Then he turned back. "I'm sorry he gave you such a fright today."

Abby thought of the Parson's soulless eyes and rubbed her arms, suddenly chilled. "He's a frightening man. I hope I never see him again."

"I'll talk to Nick and make certain that you don't."

She brushed an invisible piece of lint off her skirt to keep from meeting James's gaze. "I'm sorry. I don't know what got into me. I don't usually kiss strange men."

"I'm not a strange man," he said softly, "I'm your friend."

"I meant, a man other than my fiancé."

He walked toward her, his dark eyes warm. "I suppose I should be sorry that I kissed you, but I'm not."

Her heart started its traitorous hammering. She swallowed hard and looked at him. "I shouldn't have kissed you back."

He stood before her, his eyes holding a challenge. "Then why did you?"

"We'd both come through an emotionally charged situation, and I got caught up in the moment. I wasn't thinking clearly. Please forgive me."

"There's nothing to forgive."

She smoothed her skirt. "I think I'll go upstairs and study for a little while until Josie gets home. If you want to borrow my books and notes later . . ."

"I'll need to, since mine are probably scattered all over the campus by now."

Abby crossed the parlor. When she came to the door, she turned. "I'm glad you told me about Nick and your mother."

A faint smile touched his mouth. "I've kept that secret locked away inside for far too long. It felt good to finally share it with someone. I'm glad it was you."

She was moved that he'd chosen to confide his deepest, darkest secret to her.

Abby left him standing near the window, staring out into the street, alone with his thoughts.

It wasn't until she walked inside her own bedroom that she realized she hadn't thought about Kyle when James kissed her.

Not once.

James watched groups of exhausted factory workers trudge home to their apartments after a hard day of mindless, monotonous work while the events of the afternoon played over and over in his mind. He could still feel the panic-stricken pounding of his heart while he watched helplessly as Abby climbed into Nick's automobile and the Parson closed the door behind her.

Chasing the automobile as it drove away, James had known Nick was behind this, and he cursed his father for putting Abby in a situation where she'd relive her worst nightmare, the one that woke her screaming in the middle of the night. He couldn't begin to imagine the terror she must have been experiencing.

When his horse-drawn cab finally pulled up in front of Nick's house, James had been livid with a mixture of rage and desperation. What did Nick want with Abby?

By the time James burst in on them having tea in the study, he couldn't think straight. His self-control vanished, swamped by a rage so great, only physical violence would spend it. He hit Nick as much to punish him for taking Abby as to assuage his own anger and sense of helplessness.

Of course Nick delighted in telling Abby that James was his son. He'd dreaded the inevitable moment, imagining her recoiling in disgust when she eventually learned that that man she'd brought home to her family at Christmas was the son of a notorious criminal.

But she hadn't. She'd been magnificent. She'd stood up to Nick with as much backbone as James's mother. If Abby had been shocked by Nick's deliberate revelation, she didn't show it.

A sharp meow intruded on James's thoughts. He turned away from the window to see Ulysses perched motionless on the wooden arm of the chair, and staring at him out of those enigmatic green eyes.

"You always knew I had bad Nick Flynn blood in me, didn't you," he said. "That's why you scratched me the first day we met."

For what seemed like an eternity, the cat remained as still as the china figurine James had given Abby for

Christmas. Then he jumped down from the chair and trotted across the carpet, his skinny tail held high. When he reached James, he rubbed his body sinuously back and forth against James's leg while purring loudly.

James didn't move. He stared down at the cat weaving back and forth, leaving his scent on James's trouser leg, marking him as his property.

Then Ulysses stopped and looked up at him with a regal, demanding stare, as if to say, "Why aren't you petting me?"

James glanced down at the hand this contrary cat had once clawed. The scratches had long disappeared. He looked at Ulysses, now standing stretched up on his hind legs with his front paws resting on James's knee.

"Pardon me if I suspect your motives, but we haven't exactly been friends."

Since the cat obviously wanted to let bygones be bygones, who was James to hold a grudge? He reached down and petted him. Ulysses closed his eyes and purred as loudly as he ever had for Abby.

Realizing he was taking a big risk, James reached down and picked up the cat, taking care to support his hind legs with his left hand, while his right held his chest between the front legs. He cradled him in his arms, burying his fingers in the soft, thick fur. Ulysses didn't stiffen, or flatten his ears back against his head, or growl. He didn't bite or scratch. He patted James's cheek lightly with one front paw, his sharp claws sheathed, the pads rough against James's skin.

"You don't care if I am Nick Flynn's son, do you?"

Any more than Abby did.

Another reason why he loved her.

When James had confessed his deepest, darkest secret,

and Abby hadn't turned away in revulsion, she'd won his heart forever.

He loved her.

He'd give her the world.

He'd even die for her.

"There's only one problem," he told Ulysses. "She loves someone else."

She hadn't been thinking of Lambert when James kissed her. If she had, she would surely have resisted him and skinned him alive afterward for daring to take such liberties.

Both the tension of facing Nick and unburdening himself to Abby had demolished any lingering determination to resist her. When she had hugged him impulsively, the innocent, comforting gesture had been the final straw. He had to kiss her, Kyle Lambert be damned.

What had he told Maddy and Lizzie, that he'd never try to take what belonged to another? He rubbed his cheek against the cat's head. "I guess I'm no better than Nick after all."

He carried Ulysses upstairs to his room and opened the door. He set him down on the floor, and watched as he stalked over to his favorite mousehole and hunkered down just out of sight, waiting patiently for the scrabble of tiny claws and the appearance of a tiny whiskered nose poking out of the hole. Then he would pounce.

James smiled. "Happy hunting, General."

He'd made a new friend today.

At least something had gone right.

Abby sat at her desk with an infectious-diseases textbook open in front of her, but she hadn't turned the page since she sat down to study.

She couldn't stop thinking about the kiss.

The afternoon's events at Flynn's had placed both her and James under a great deal of strain. They both had suffered from a momentary lapse in judgment. They had kissed, but it was a chaste kiss between friends, nothing more.

She closed her book and rose. Who was she trying to convince? Chaste kiss indeed. He'd kissed her with passion and desire, as she'd never been kissed before—even by Kyle.

She'd enjoyed feeling James's hard, strong arms around her. He made her feel cherished and protected. His mouth, both so gentle and forceful, stirred her physically and left her breathless. She shivered at the memory.

Memories of Kyle's kisses had never made her shiver.

What was happening to her? She was engaged to Kyle, yet here she was, having wanton, improper thoughts about James.

Abby reached for the cat figurine that she kept high on a shelf where Ulysses couldn't climb and knock it off. She took James's Christmas gift over to the window seat and sat down. She turned it this way and that, admiring the craftsmanship, the detail, right down to the enigmatic green eyes.

She could picture him going through shop after crowded shop during the Christmas season, looking for the perfect gift for her, one with meaning.

A tiny spark of light bouncing off her ring made her think of Kyle. She loved him. She wanted a future with him. Didn't she?

Abby twisted the ring until she hid the stone and only the band showed like a wedding ring. Soon she'd graduate. She and James would go their separate ways. She'd return home to Little Falls and marry Kyle. James would find some town where he could open his veterinary practice and buy a farm. Perhaps she'd receive a letter or two in the beginning, and a card at Christmas. Then they'd stop. She'd never hear from him again. Her life would go on.

She sat back and closed her eyes. She thought of herself and Kyle in the barn last summer, when they'd come so close to making love. His intimate touching and caressing had paled in comparison to James's simple kiss.

She wondered what would have happened if she and James hadn't stopped with a kiss.

Abby took a deep, shuddering breath to quell the emotions that suddenly swamped her. She mustn't think about James in those terms. She mustn't think of him as a potential lover.

She kept telling herself that she loved Kyle.

Abby rose and returned the figurine to its shelf. She looked down at her book in consternation. She couldn't study. Pointless to even try. She might as well let James borrow her books.

She collected her books and notes and went down the hall to his room. She noticed he'd left his door open. She paused in the doorway.

James was sitting at his desk, staring at Lizzie's watercolor landscape.

There sat Ulysses at his favorite mousehole.

Abby gasped. The sound made James turn in his chair. "I'm sorry," she said, walking into the room and heading for her cat. "He must've snuck in again. I'll have him out in a second."

James rose. "Leave him."

Abby stopped and stared. "I thought you didn't want Ulysses in your room."

He smiled. "We've made peace, and we're best

friends now. He can come in my room any time.''

Kyle had never tried to make friends with Ulysses when she brought him home for the summer.

She smiled. ''Harmony has been restored to the boardinghouse.''

As she handed James her books, their fingers touched. Abby felt a jolt of awareness shoot up her arm. James must have felt something too, for he quickly took the books and set them on his desk.

Abby sensed another kind of tension slowly filling the house ever since their kiss.

The following afternoon after James's last class, he paid another visit to Nick.

When he arrived, he hugged a whining, wriggling, overjoyed Moriarty, who would have licked his face off if given half the chance, indicating that he'd forgiven James for being so sharp with him the previous day.

Then, unsure of his welcome after yesterday's fiasco, James had Gardiner announce him.

Three of Nick's unsavory ''business associates'' were leaving the study just as James walked through the double doors, and he gave the men wide berth. He found his usually fastidious father sitting coatless and tieless at his desk, his shirtsleeves rolled up almost to the elbows. A purplish bruise marked his jaw.

Nick looked up at him. No animosity darkened his icy blue eyes. ''I've killed men for less.''

''I know, but I'm your son, as you delight in reminding me.''

Nick smiled, then grimaced and swore. ''You pack a mean punch, kid.''

James walked up to the desk. ''You deserved it for interfering in my life when I've repeatedly warned you not to." He placed his hands on the desk and leaned forward. "And scaring my friend half to death."

Nick raised his black, flaring brows. "*Friend*, you say. I'd say Miss Cooper is more than a *friend*, my boy."

"I told you I'm not sleeping with her."

"But you want to."

Yes, he wanted to. So badly he'd spent most of the night in sheer physical agony.

"We don't always get what we want in life," he said, straightening.

"Sure we do," Nick replied. "If we're willing to take it."

James felt his self control slipping. "Abigail Cooper isn't something you *take*."

Nick shrugged. "Then you get what you settle for."

He rose and rolled down his shirtsleeves. "What are you doing here? I thought after yesterday I'd seen the last of you."

"I want to explain the damage you could've caused by abducting Miss Cooper yesterday, and why I hit you."

While Nick poured himself a much too generous scotch, James told him about the thugs who had kidnapped Abby in the spring, and how she still had nightmares about the terrifying experience.

Nick looked repentant as he sipped his drink. "I didn't know. I sent the Parson for her because I didn't think she'd answer an engraved invitation."

James folded his arms. "Why couldn't you have just left her alone? Why'd you have to meet her at all?"

Nick sat down. "Isn't it natural for a father to want to meet the woman his only son loves?"

"I don't—"

"Don't lie to me, Jimmy," Nick snapped. "The minute you came charging through that door, I knew. You looked straight at her, and I saw fear in your eyes. You were afraid for her." He sipped his scotch. "A man doesn't act that way about a woman who's a mere *friend*."

Nick was right. James said nothing.

"I like your Miss Cooper. Not only is she beautiful, she's smart, and she's got spirit." He smiled and winced again. "Life would never be dull with a woman like that."

No, life certainly wouldn't. Not with Abby.

Nick looked at him. "So, will I be invited to the wedding? I'll sit in the back. No one will even know I'm there."

"There's not going to be a wedding," James said. "At least, not for me."

"What do you mean?"

"Abby's engaged to someone else."

17

NICK STARED AT HIM WITH DISBELIEF AND IRE. "You're letting the woman you love marry somebody else?"

James gave a contemptuous snort. "She doesn't love me. What am I supposed to do? Lock her in a room and keep her prisoner until she agrees to marry me?"

"That's barbaric. We're not living in the Dark Ages, Jimmy." Nick rose. "You do what I did with your mother. You woo her. You bring her flowers. You dine by candlelight. You shower her with jewels."

James tried, and failed, to picture a young, brash, rough Nick Flynn wooing the sophisticated, celebrated Lucille Bradshaw.

"But she didn't marry you," he pointed out.

"To my everlasting regret," Nick replied. "But we were just as married as if we'd gotten the license and gone through the ceremony."

"Abby's not the kind of woman to be impressed by flowers and expensive baubles." Though she had liked the cat figurine he had given her for Christmas.

She was more likely to love a man who made friends

with her cat. Well, he'd done that, and it hadn't worked.

"Then you make her feel like she's the most desirable woman in the world. And that you're the right man—the only man—for her."

"She's already engaged."

"What's his name and where does he live? I could have the Parson take care of him for you, like he did that Shays fellow."

James gave him a warning scowl. "Nick . . ."

"Okay, okay, I'll stay out of it. But remember, she hasn't walked down the aisle with him yet. She has time to change her mind." He made a dismissive gesture. "Women are always changing their minds. Your mother changed hers a hundred times a day. Sometimes two hundred."

James wished Abby would change her mind about Kyle Lambert.

"What did Miss Cooper say when you told her about me?" Nick's icy gaze glinted with self-deprecating amusement.

"She said it didn't matter, that just because I was the son of a criminal didn't make *me* one."

"Smart and wise, with a big heart, just like your mother. I could tell when she stood up to me." Nick walked over to his desk. "Unlike me, you're a man with scruples. And I really admire that about you, son. But don't let those scruples stand in the way of your happiness. Miss Cooper is one in a million. Fight for her, Jimmy. Don't let her get away."

He stared at his father in astonishment. Was Nick going soft? This romantic, sentimental streak was so unlike the man James knew.

Nick took a key from his watch fob, unlocked a desk drawer, and rummaged around. When he found what he was looking for, a small, square box, he relocked the drawer and walked over to James.

He held out the blue velvet box and lifted the lid. Inside was a large oval dark blue sapphire ring circled with diamonds.

"Mother's favorite ring," James said.

His throat tightened at the memory of that ring flashing on her slender hand with every expansive gesture.

Nick stared at it, his own memories softening his hard features. "I gave it to her when you were born." He proffered the box to James. "She intended for you to give it to the woman you love."

"She's already wearing another man's ring."

"She is?" he scoffed. "The stone must've been so small I didn't notice. Now *this* is a ring a woman would be proud to wear. Here. Take it. Maybe it'll help you to change Miss Cooper's mind."

James took the ring. He snapped the lid shut and pocketed the box. "As much as I hate to admit it, Mother loved you. I couldn't understand why, but I know that she did."

Nick shrugged. "She couldn't help herself. I was a catch."

James smiled in spite of himself and thanked Nick for the ring. "I'm not going to get my hopes up."

"Remember what I said. She's fair game until the day she walks down the aisle."

James rose from his desk, stood at his bedroom window, and idly looked into the street below. A young couple strolled arm in arm past the boardinghouse. They didn't look up to see James at the window, watching. They ignored several boys running home to the apartment building next door. They didn't even seem to mind the brisk April breeze that halfheartedly tried to snatch away their hats.

They had eyes only for each other.

They were obviously in love.

James turned from the window and walked away in disgust. Or was it envy?

He pulled the chair from beneath his desk, and sat down with his elbows propped on his knees, forearms dangling. He stared at the worn Turkish carpet as if relief from his torment were some secret message woven into the faded pattern.

Actually, relief from his torment dwelled right across the hall.

Abby.

James groaned. He cradled his head in his hands and ran his fingers through his hair until it stood up like spikes. He smiled grimly to himself. Perhaps he should bang his head against the wall until the pain eradicated all thoughts of her. Perhaps he should just have the Parson surprise him in a dark alley and put him out of his misery.

When he had revealed the truth about his parentage and his dark, troubled past, to Abby, and they kissed, he had sensed more barriers falling between them. They had progressed from adversaries to friends. He had hoped they would become more than friends. But it hadn't happened.

He knew why. Abby loved Kyle Lambert and planned to marry him. She did not love James Bradshaw. She was too principled to even allow herself to be tempted by another man. He supposed he should admire her for such devotion.

Oh, she may have experienced a momentary lapse and gotten caught up in the moment when he kissed her. The

Ice Maiden, as he had discovered to his delight, possessed a soul of fire. Just one kiss, and James was ready to burn with her forever. Once they parted and sanity returned, Abby retreated behind her wall of iron self-control.

The fire went out. She acted as though the kiss had never happened.

They walked to school together. They attended classes together. They returned to the boardinghouse. They dined with Josie. They studied. Just as they always had.

They never discussed the kiss.

He wondered if she ever thought about it. He suspected she did. Sometimes he caught her staring at him when she thought he wasn't looking, and her expression was definitely speculative.

Was she wondering what it would be like to become his lover?

He often felt tempted to force the issue with her, but that was Nick's method, not his. He wouldn't—couldn't—take what belonged to another.

So James studied even harder, until he thought his brain couldn't hold the details of one more veterinary procedure. He still hoped to become valedictorian, but Abby remained ahead of him academically, though the gap was narrowing.

A plaintive meow disturbed James's thoughts. He looked over to see Ulysses sitting not two feet away, his head cocked to the side as if trying to divine James's thoughts.

He sat up straight in his chair. The cat jumped into his lap, turned around twice, then tucked his paws beneath him and settled in. James gently petted him, soothing himself as well as the cat.

"You know that your mistress is driving me insane," he said.

Ulysses yawned and closed his eyes. He didn't want to hear it. He just wanted to be cosseted.

James obliged, until he had the cat purring beneath his slow hand. He smiled wryly. He wondered if Abby would purr if he caressed her. He would see to it that she did.

His smile died abruptly when a thought occurred to him. What if Abby was resisting him because she and her fiancé were already lovers? The commitment of sexual intimacy would be a powerful, unbreakable bond for a woman like Abby. She wouldn't give herself to a man casually, but once she did, she would belong to him body and soul.

Graphic images of Kyle Lambert kissing, caressing, possessing Abby sent shards of anger and jealousy straight to James's heart. He cursed through gritted teeth and bolted to his feet, momentarily forgetting the cat curled in his lap.

Ulysses yowled in protest as he was unceremoniously dumped, but like all cats, he landed surely on his feet. Once the shock wore off, he shook himself and sauntered out of the room without a backward glance.

But James had forgotten all about the cat. In another few days, Abby would be leaving to spend spring break in Little Falls. Once she returned, they would have only a few more weeks of school before final exams and graduation.

Then they would go their separate ways.

James would never see her again.

He couldn't allow that. He had to declare his love before it was too late.

• • •

"Abby, wake up."

She opened her eyes with a start, expecting to see a fearsome Kyle seated across from her once again in the golden carriage. The panic receded when she recognized the familiar surroundings of her bedroom in the boardinghouse. A concerned-looking Josie stood beside Abby's bed. James hovered behind their landlady, his expression alert.

"You must've had a bad dream," Josie said with a kindly smile. "But it's over now. You're safe and sound."

"We heard your scream," James said.

Abby took several deep breaths to calm her shivers. At least she hadn't broken out in the cold sweat of fear. She managed a tremulous smile. "I had a nightmare, but I'm fine."

James's dark eyes held worry. "The same one you had in Little Falls over Christmas?"

She remembered hearing his voice outside her bedroom door, asking her mother if she was all right. "The same."

Josie patted her hand. "Well, you get back to sleep, my dear. You need your rest."

When Josie and James left and closed the door behind them, Abby lay in the darkness, staring at the ceiling. Ulysses, who'd been watching her from the foot of the bed, walked across the coverlet to curl up at her side.

She petted him, taking comfort in his warmth and unconditional love.

Her second nightmare about Kyle abducting her in a golden carriage. Why did she dream about him as one of her abductors? He wasn't an evil man. He loved her. She loved him.

Abby tossed and turned for a few minutes. When she

couldn't get back to sleep, she rose, put on her robe, and went downstairs to the kitchen to make herself a cup of hot milk.

No sooner did she set the pan of milk on the stove than a voice said, "Can't sleep?"

She started, then turned to see James standing in the doorway in his bathrobe, looking mussed and rumpled.

"That's why I came down to make some hot milk," she replied. "It usually helps me sleep. Would you like a cup?"

"Thanks." He walked into the kitchen, sat down at the table, and rubbed the sleep from his eyes like a little boy just waking from a long afternoon nap.

Abby found the gesture oddly touching. She stirred the milk with a wooden spoon to make sure it didn't scorch.

"You've never had the nightmare here in the board-inghouse, have you?" he said.

She kept stirring. "Odd, isn't it? Though I was abducted in Chicago, I only have the nightmare when I'm in Little Falls." She didn't tell him about the addition of Kyle and the golden carriage.

"That is odd," he agreed, leaning back in his chair. "After my parents and I were almost assassinated, I had nightmares about it for several years."

She glanced over her shoulder. There was something about sitting in a kitchen in the middle of the night, sharing a cup of hot milk, to ease the inhibitions and reveal secrets.

"Every time I saw a rough-looking stranger," he said, "I wondered if he was concealing a gun. Every time my mother dressed to go out to the theater or to a concert, I wondered if she'd be coming home." He shook his head. "Life with Nick."

"After I was abducted," Abby said, "every time a carriage drove past slowly, I panicked. If I saw two men walking together toward me, I'd cross the street."

Bubbles were forming around the edge of the milk, so Abby poured the steaming liquid into two of Josie's Chicago Exposition souvenir cups, and brought them over to the table. She set hers down at her place. When she handed the other in her right hand to James and he reached to take it, his fingers brushed against hers, leaving a trail of fire.

Startled, she let go of the cup before James quite gripped it. The cup crashed to the table and broke. The long sleeves of Abby's kimono offered some protection against the scalding liquid, but a few drops still managed to splash against the inside of Abby's tender wrist.

She cried out in a mixture of surprise and pain, and jerked her hand away.

James rose. "Are you all right?" he demanded, his deep voice tight with urgency and apprehension as he rounded the table. "Were you burned?"

"Not badly," she replied, regarding the slowly spreading puddle of spilled milk in dismay. "A few drops hit my wrist, that's all. It's nothing. I'll be fine."

She turned to find a cloth to mop up the spill, when James suddenly caught her hand. She looked at him quizzically.

He turned her hand palm up. The kimono's wide sleeve slid halfway down her forearm, baring her wrist. He raised her hand to examine her pinkening skin more closely.

Those onyx eyes held hers in an unblinking stare. "Does it hurt?"

"Just stings."

An expectant hush fell like a thick blanket on the

dimly lit kitchen. The outside world ceased to exist, swallowed by the blackest of nights. Only Abby and James remained.

His gaze never leaving hers, he drew her hand to his mouth and kissed the throbbing pulse in her sensitive inner wrist. His warm, soft lips soothed her stinging flesh better than any of Josie's ointments. She shivered in spite of the kitchen's warmth.

It's happening again, she thought. *Run from him while you still can.*

Too late.

"Cold?" he whispered.

No. In danger.

She shook her head, unable to tear her gaze away from that handsome, tormented face. She wanted to, but she couldn't.

He lowered her hand to his side, but didn't release it. He studied her thoughtfully, as though trying to make up his mind about something.

"Don't go to Little Falls for spring break," he said. "Stay here. With me."

"I have to go," she replied. "Kyle and I—"

"To hell with Kyle," he said, his gaze searing her. "You don't belong with Kyle. You belong with me." He took a deep breath. "I love you, you know."

Had she just heard James Bradshaw say that he loved her, or was she still upstairs, dreaming?

She stepped back, but he didn't release her hand. "You can't be serious."

"I've never been more serious in my life. I love you." A wry smile touched his mouth. "I can't say that I've loved you from the very first moment I saw you, because I'd be lying. It snuck up on me by surprise."

Abby took another step back, gently breaking his hold

on her hand. Why did she still feel as if some invisible cord still bound them? "I'm flattered, but you know I'm already spoken for."

"Haven't you ever wondered how you and I would be together?"

She had, at Christmas, when Lizzie had speculated about painting James in the nude, and Abby had become so jealous. But she couldn't tell him that.

"You're a good friend," she said.

"I want to be more than a good friend," he said. "I want to be your lover. And your husband, if you'll have me."

She stared at him as if he'd gone mad. A marriage proposal from James Bradshaw. "I can't marry you. I'm going to marry Kyle."

"Do you love him?"

"You know I do."

His eyes narrowed. "How do you know you love him? I've never heard you talk about your courtship, or how you two fell in love?"

"We—we just did," Abby sputtered. Even as she said the words, she realized her reason sounded more like an excuse.

James's eyes sparkled, whether from love or desperation, Abby couldn't tell. "Spend spring break with me. Give me a chance to prove my love to you. Give yourself a chance to see how good we are for each other."

"I can't. That would be betraying Kyle."

"Just a week. That's all I'm asking. Once the time is over, if you decide that we don't belong together, the issue will be settled."

One week with James. Abby was sorely tempted. But she knew deep in her heart that if she spent the week with this compelling, seductive man, she'd never go back to Kyle.

"Engagements are broken every day," he said. "You can return his ring and tell him you're sorry, but that you've fallen in love with someone else. Simple."

Abby hesitated, impossibly torn. She and Kyle loved each other and had made such plans for their future. She had pledged her troth to him, and she couldn't break her promise, even if she was so drawn to James.

"I love Kyle," she said.

James frowned slightly as he studied her. "I can't understand what you see in him. Neither can Lizzie. She told me that Lambert was about as exciting as watching milk curdle. She said you needed a man who would challenge you."

Abby's slumbering temper awakened. "Sometimes Lizzie doesn't know when to keep her unwanted opinions to herself."

"She only wants what's best for you. As do I."

"And you think you're what's best for me."

"I know I am, but you're bound and determined to keep me from proving it to you." He reached out and cradled her face between his palms, gently stroking her cheeks with the pads of his thumbs. "At Christmas, when I realized that I loved you, I thought I'd go mad when Lambert gave you that ring."

He released her, only to reach down for her left hand. He glared at her ring as if it were a flesh and blood rival. "I wanted you, but it was too late. Another man had just claimed you."

Abby remembered the shuttered emptiness in James's eyes when he'd come up to offer his best wishes on her engagement. She could tell something was bothering him. Another man had gotten what he wanted.

"Take his ring off," he whispered. He brushed his lips across her knuckles in the lightest of kisses that made Abby's heart pound. "Give me a chance. Give yourself a chance. Just a week. That's all I ask."

She drew her hand away and closed it into a loose fist to keep Kyle's ring on her finger where it belonged. "I'm sorry, but I can't love you, James. Spending a week with you—spending a year with you—won't change that."

A slow, seductive smile warmed his eyes with a devilish light. "The way you kissed me after we returned from Nick's told me otherwise."

A faint blush warmed her cheeks. She looked away. "You were in such pain, and I only meant to comfort you."

"That was more than a comforting kiss, and you know it."

Suddenly the light went out of his eyes. "Is it because I'm Nick Flynn's son? Are you afraid I'll turn into a monster?"

Abby stiffened, her eyes widening. "I'm appalled that you could even think such a thing! You're nothing like your father. I can't love you because I love another, James. That's the one and *only* reason."

He closed his eyes and let out a long, defeated sigh. "I've done my best to convince you, but you refuse to admit your feelings for me. I can't do any more." He stepped back a pace. "I'm going to move out of the boardinghouse. When you return from Little Falls, I'll be gone."

Abby stared at him. "But why? You like living here. It's close to the college, the rent is cheap, and Josie is a wonderful cook."

He shocked her by gripping her shoulders hard, and

giving them a little shake, forcing her to look at him. "Why? Because I'm not some damn eunuch. Living in the same house with you, seeing you every day, loving you the way I do and not being able to touch you . . ." His hands fell away. "A man can take only so much, and I've reached the end of my rope."

Abby didn't know what to say.

"It's late," he said. "We have classes tomorrow, and we both need our rest."

He gave her one last determined look, wished her good night, and left.

After mopping up the milk, Abby returned to her bedroom, agitated and unable to sleep. She gathered Ulysses into her arms and sat at the window seat.

She tried to tell herself that James's passionate declaration had shocked and surprised her, but that wasn't entirely the truth. She had sensed something building between them ever since she'd found out about his father.

James had trusted her. He had exposed his darkest fear, revealed a thread of vulnerability running through his strength. Abby hadn't turned away from him. She'd reached out to share her own strength.

James had mistaken her comfort for love.

Or did she really love him, and refused to admit it, even to herself? Fresh doubts and misgivings assailed her.

Abby knew Lizzie didn't think Kyle was exciting. His courtship hadn't swept Abby off her feet and sent her spinning among the stars. Kyle had presented himself as an ambitious young man with a future, who'd be honored to have her as his wife. They certainly didn't share a love of veterinary medicine, or her cat.

But there was something solid and steadfast about their relationship, and if it lacked both the intellectual and physical excitement that Abby always felt in James's presence, she'd find other compensations.

She petted her cat. Was she making a mistake by not taking James up on his offer and spending spring break with him? She couldn't. She'd made a commitment to Kyle, and she'd honor it, even if she was making the biggest mistake of her life.

On the first day of spring break, James left the boardinghouse early while Abby was bathing. He had no intention of seeing her off at the train station later that morning, or saying good-bye.

He went to Nick's, and for the first time in his life, swallowed his pride and asked his father for a favor. Actually, the favor was for Abby. He hoped it brought her peace.

He spent the rest of the day in the city, strolling down Lake Shore Drive, taking a steamer out on Lake Michigan, shopping at Marshall Field's, where he bought several new cups for Josie to replace the one Abby had broken the night she'd made them hot milk.

Then he returned to the boardinghouse and broke the news to Josie that he would be moving out by the end of the week.

When Abby returned from Little Falls, she'd find him gone.

18

MONDAY, APRIL 25, WAS THE DAY FESTUS DOBBS intended to catch the culprit who kept breaking into his barn's storeroom. Not that anything was ever missing, just moved around. To a meticulous man like Festus who had a place for everything and wanted to see everything in its place, preferably in the mercantile, the intruder's forays would not be tolerated.

He had to be unmasked. Exposed.

Festus suspected that rapscallion Blick boy, Helmut. Always getting into trouble. After he broke the mercantile's window last summer and his father made him pay for it out of his allowance, the boy had it in for the Dobbs family. Festus knew his revenge would be subtle. This time, he wouldn't leave any evidence of wrongdoing.

What better way to get revenge than by moving items around in the storeroom and making old Festus think he was going crazy?

His son and daughter-in-law thought he was making a mountain out of a molehill. According to his granddaughter Mary, he had too much time on his hands.

He'd show them.

So he slipped out of the house at the crack of dawn and went out to the barn in back of the mercantile.

The carriage horse stared at him, obviously surprised to see him this early, then closed its eyes and went back to sleep. Festus went into the storeroom, left the door slightly ajar, and hunkered down behind a sack of grain to wait.

He didn't have to wait long.

He heard the old barn door creak as someone opened and closed it.

Then he heard voices, one a woman's, light and soft, followed by a man's deeper tones. Festus listened with all his might, but his hearing wasn't as sharp as it used to be, and damned if he could place them.

They sure didn't sound anything like the Blick boy.

Festus held his breath and waited. Any minute now, they'd come into the storeroom. And get the surprise of their lives.

Minutes passed.

No sign of them.

Festus frowned in the darkness. He would have heard the barn door creak if they'd left. They must still be in here.

A high, keening cry rent the silence.

Festus froze, his eyes widening.

He stood up and crept over to the storeroom door. He opened it slowly, its well-oiled hinges merely whispering. He stepped into the outer barn. Now he recognized the sounds that he guessed were coming from one of the empty box stalls.

He grinned. He and his late wife Tessie had sounded exactly like that on their wedding night.

He hesitated. Maybe he should leave the lovers alone.

No, this barn was private property. If a couple wanted to fornicate, let them do so in their own bedroom.

They were moaning and groaning so enthusiastically Festus doubted if they'd hear a herd of horses come charging by. He walked up to the stall and peered over the closed door.

If he'd had a weak heart, the shock of what he saw would surely have killed him.

"We have some bad news for you," Cat said, reaching for Abby's hands and holding them tightly.

Abby had been surprised to step off the train and find both her parents waiting for her on the station platform. Usually her father came alone.

Panic gripped her. "Is it Grandmama Maddy?" Before either parent could reply, she blurted out, "Something's happened to Grandpapa Jace."

"No, no, it's nothing like that, puss," Michael said. "Everybody's fine."

Cat shot him an angry glance. "Everybody except Kyle."

Abby's heart stopped.

"Kyle?" She grasped her mother's hands tightly, and looked from one parent to the other. "Is he sick? Did he have an accident? Is he *dead*?" Her voice rose hysterically. "Damn it, will one of you please tell me what in God's name is going *on*?"

Cat released her hands, grabbed her shoulders, and gave her a little shake. "Abigail, get a hold of yourself. Kyle isn't sick, and he didn't have an accident."

"But he's gonna wish he was dead," Michael muttered under his breath.

"Mama—"

"Let's go. There's no privacy here. We'll tell you in the surrey."

Abby forced herself to be patient as she followed her parents to the surrey. She waited while her father loaded her suitcase, and once she and her mother were seated, he took the reins and they started back to Little Falls.

Cat twisted in her seat. "There's no easy way to break bad news except to come right out and say it." She took a deep breath. "Kyle has been unfaithful to you, puss."

Abby rolled her eyes. "Oh, Mama, don't tell me you believe those lies about Kyle going upstairs with the saloon girls. Because he doesn't. He swore to me."

"No, he doesn't go upstairs with the saloon girls," her mother said. "He's been going out to the Dobbs's barn with Mary."

Abby grew very still and stared at her in disbelief. "What did you say?"

"You heard me."

"It's true," Michael added heavily. "Festus caught them going at it yesterday morning."

Kyle in the barn with Mary.

Impossible.

"I don't believe it." She swallowed hard and stared down at her engagement ring, the tangible symbol of their love. "Festus is mistaken. It couldn't have been Kyle. Just because he felt sorry for her and bought Mary's box lunch at the Harvest Festival doesn't mean he—"

"Abby, Festus knows Kyle," Cat pointed out with maddening logic. "And he knows his own granddaughter."

"Even without her clothes," her father added.

"Michael, please," Cat snapped. "This is difficult enough."

He glanced back over his shoulder and muttered an apology.

Abby shook her head and stared doggedly ahead. "Kyle wouldn't do that to me. He loves me. We're going to get married."

"I'm afraid not." Her mother's eyes were bright with sympathy and shared pain. "Mary is going to have a baby."

A baby.

Abby felt as though the sky had caved in, the heavy clouds crushing her. "Just because she's going to have a baby doesn't mean that Kyle's the father."

"She says he is," Cat said.

"Then she's lying," Abby insisted. "It must be another man's, and she's using his child to try to trap Kyle."

Her father shook his head. "I wish to God that were true, for your sake, Abby, but Kyle isn't denying it."

She looked from her father to her mother. "He's not?"

"He's not," Cat said.

Abby said, "How far along is she?"

"Dr. Kendall estimates three months."

Three months.

Each word sank like a stone being thrown into a pond, and the ramifications rippled out through Abby's consciousness. If Mary was pregnant, yesterday wasn't the first time she and Kyle had been lying together. They must have been making secret trips to the Dobbs's barn since after Christmas.

A lie. His declarations of love had all been a lie.

She looked at her mother sitting there, watching her. She swallowed hard. "It's true, then."

"We're not making this up to hurt you, puss," Cat

said. "I know the family never approved of Kyle, but we were hoping he'd prove us wrong. For your sake."

Instead, he had proven them right.

Damn him.

Abby took a deep breath. "What happened after Festus . . ." She couldn't say it.

"All hell broke loose," Michael said. "Mary was crying and begging him not to tell her parents, but Festus was outraged that Kyle had taken advantage of his granddaughter. By the time Festus got his son and they went back out to the barn, Kyle and Mary were both dressed and denying anything had happened."

Abby's lip curled in disgust. He couldn't even face the music.

Cat rubbed her forehead. "Mary's parents had her examined by Dr. Kendall, and he discovered she's pregnant."

"So the Dobbses are insisting that Kyle make an honest woman of her," Michael said.

Abby looked out of dull, unseeing eyes at the countryside awakening to spring. How she wished it were still winter and as cold and bitter as she felt in her heart.

She absently twisted her engagement ring. "Kyle has agreed to marry her?"

"At first he refused," Cat said, "because he insisted he loves you and wants to marry you. He said that if the child was his, he'd support it, but he said he knew you'd understand, and that you'd stick by him."

Abby shuddered in revulsion. As if she'd ever marry a man who betrayed her trust and fathered a child by another woman.

Cat's blue eyes darkened with contempt. "Then the Dobbses offered to buy him the saloon."

Abby recoiled from this latest blow with a groan.

"Tell me he didn't agree to marry Mary if her parents bought him the saloon."

Her mother didn't have to say a word. Abby could read the answer written plainly on her face.

"I can't believe it," she muttered, her disillusionment so complete she felt as though a herd of horses had trampled her. "I can't believe he'd betray me for the saloon."

Her thoughts returned to Christmas, when Kyle had asked her if her parents were planning to give them the saloon for their wedding. Why, the cad had been planning and scheming to use her even then. And she had been too much in love—or too much of a fool—to see it.

Her father stared straight ahead. "Better to find out now what kind of man he is than later, after you're married, puss."

Abby sat back in her seat. Her eyes felt dry and hot. She couldn't even cry, her devastation and her wounds cut so deep.

She wished James were here.

She looked over at her mother. "I suppose the whole town is buzzing about what he did. Grandmama Maddy. Regina." Lizzie didn't know yet, but Abby knew her sister wouldn't be surprised when she heard the news.

Cat nodded.

"I must be the town laughingstock," Abby said.

Beautiful, intelligent Abigail Cooper, jilted for plain Mary Dobbs. Well, Mary obviously had some quality Abby lacked to keep Kyle coming back for more.

"No," Michael said. "You're the injured party. No one's laughing at you, believe me."

Abby felt hot tears sting her eyes. "Why did he have

to do this, Mama? We were going to be so happy together.''

"I don't know, baby," Cat said gently. "I just don't know."

When they arrived in Little Falls, Abby's father stopped the surrey at the far end of Main Street and turned in his seat. "Are you sure you want to confront him now?"

"Yes, Papa," she replied, tight-lipped and determined. "I want to get this over with."

"Why don't we go home first?" Cat suggested. "Give yourself some time to rest, time to think about what happened. Time to plan what you're going to say to Kyle."

"I don't need any time to think about what happened," Abby replied. She had spent the last agonizing hour doing just that. "I know exactly what I'm going to say to that low-down, lying snake."

Her father gave her a smile of encouragement. "That's my girl."

He lifted the reins and clucked to the horse.

As the surrey rolled down Main Street, Abby sat straight and proud beside her mother, looking neither right nor left—until they approached the mercantile and she saw Mary out front, sweeping the boardwalk.

Abby stared daggers at her, willing Mary to raise her head and look back. She did. When their gazes met and locked for what seemed like a lifetime, Mary turned a guilty shade of scarlet and quickly returned to her sweeping. She didn't look at Abby again.

Abby took little enjoyment from Mary's humiliation. The shame would fade with time, but Mary was having Kyle's baby, and now she had Abby's man.

The surrey stopped in front of One-Eyed Jack's.

Abby stepped down and with her head held high, glided inside.

"Where is he?" she said to Minnie, polishing the bar.

"In his office," Minnie replied.

Abby headed for the back, then stopped. "Will you answer one question for me?"

Minnie stopped polishing. "What do you want to know?"

"Did he ever go upstairs with any of you girls?"

Minnie said nothing, but her guilty look spoke volumes.

When Abby came to Kyle's closed office door, she paused, but only long enough to take a deep breath and compose herself. She opened the door without knocking, and stepped inside.

He was seated at his desk, with his back to the door. He didn't swivel around right away, just said, "I hope it's Mary."

"Mary is still sweeping the mercantile's boardwalk."

Kyle swung his chair around and rose to face her. Abby searched his handsome face for any sign of regret or remorse or even embarrassment. Nothing. He didn't even have the grace to bow his head in shame when confronted by the woman whose trust he'd betrayed.

He merely looked peeved. "Your parents just couldn't wait to tell you, could they?"

"They love me and care about me. Which is more than I can say for you."

"But I do love you, Abby."

She raised her brows. "Is that why you were rutting in the barn with Mary while I was away at school?"

He scowled. "What do you expect? I'm a man, with a man's needs. If you hadn't left me to go to Chicago, I never would've turned to Mary."

Abby's Irish temper exploded. "I didn't go to Chicago to leave you, Kyle Lambert. I went to Chicago to attend veterinary school."

"That's all you ever thought about, isn't it? Your precious veterinary school. What about *my* dream of owning my own business? You didn't care about that. Every time I asked if your precious family could help me out financially, you turned deaf. They'd paid for your education, and that's all that mattered."

"And all that ever mattered to you was getting my parents to buy you Jack's. Did it ever occur to you to work hard and buy it yourself? Once we were married and I was a practicing vet, we could've afforded it. It might've taken a little longer, but—"

"You see, that's the difference between you and Mary. She's a real woman, who understands a real man's ambition. She knows how much Jack's means to me. You never did."

Abby shook her head. "Poor Mary. Does she know you're marrying her because her parents are bribing you?"

"I prefer to think of Jack's as her dowry. And of course she knows it. She's the one who suggested it. She and her parents know she's too plain to get a man any other way."

Abby raised her brows. "What a kind, sensitive thing to say about the woman you're going to marry, the mother of your child."

He shrugged. "I'm not saying anything folks don't already know. And as for the kid, what about it? As long as I get what I want, she can have what she wants. We're both happy."

Abby knew that Mary would be raising an illegitimate child on her own if her parents hadn't come through with the saloon. Kyle would have turned his back on her and his responsibilities in the blink of an eye.

He smiled lasciviously. "And I'll tell you something else. Mary may be as plain as a plank, but she's got a sweet, shapely body just made for loving. When it comes to pleasing a man in bed, she learns fast."

Abby's lip curled. "You're disgusting. What did I ever see in you?"

He leaned his large frame against his desk and gripped the sides, displaying himself for her. "You *would* think I'm disgusting. That's because you're an icicle. You couldn't get a man hot if somebody set you on fire first."

Abby glowered at him. "That's not what you said last summer in my grandmother's barn when you tried to take liberties with me."

He shrugged. "I just did that to see how far you'd go. The minute you heard your grandmother calling, you stopped me quick enough."

"You saved me from making the biggest mistake of my life, so I suppose I should thank you."

"You always did look down your high-and-mighty Cooper nose at my running a saloon. All this talk of my getting rid of the girls."

Abby's anger rose again, burning hot and fierce. "Just one minute, Kyle Lambert. You're the one who told me that you'd be getting rid of the girls once we were married and you bought Jack's."

"That was only to appease your family so they'd approve of our marriage. Mary doesn't care if the girls go or stay. She just cares about *me*."

"Maybe she'll care when you go trotting upstairs with them to sample the wares," Abby snapped. "Oh, don't look so affronted. I may've been blinded by love, but I'm not stupid."

"No, you've always been too smart for your own good," he said with a regretful sigh. "Men don't like women who are too smart."

"James Bradshaw does."

Kyle's expression darkened. "So, you have been whoring around with him in that boardinghouse."

"As difficult as you may find this to believe, we're just friends."

"I don't find that hard to believe at all. You're so cold, the thought of giving yourself to any man scares you silly."

Was he right? When she'd gone down to the kitchen to make herself some hot milk, and James had kissed her wrist and declared himself, she'd pulled away. Was it really because she loved Kyle, or did she fear becoming intimate with a man?

Kyle folded his arms across his chest. "You'll have your fancy education and you'll become a veterinarian, but you'll never become a real woman. You'll wind up sharing your life with that damned cat."

She smiled. "I'll take a cat over a rat any day."

Kyle glowered at her, suddenly at a loss for words as her barb hit home.

Abby turned to go. "Give Mary all my best. She's going to need it."

Kyle cleared his throat. "Abby, wait a minute."

She stopped and turned.

"The ring. I need it back to give to Mary."

Abby pulled the ring off her finger and squinted at the small stone before she threw his meaningless love token back at him.

Then she turned and left him cursing her and crawling around on the floor.

● ● ●

Abby trotted Fireworks through the fields, enjoying her last day of spring break. Tomorrow she'd be heading back to Chicago.

She was glad to be going. She was tired of all the sympathic looks and encouragement she'd been receiving from the townsfolk the few times she did ride into Little Falls to see her grandmother or sister. She deliberately stayed out of the mercantile.

Though she tried to tell herself she was better off without Kyle, she couldn't deny that his rejection had left her feeling weak and vulnerable. She'd always thought of herself as beautiful and desirable, and yet Kyle had left her for a woman who couldn't get a man unless her parents bought her one.

She petted Fireworks's arched neck. Was she as cold and unfeeling as Kyle claimed?

She thought of James, and she felt a heavy weight of regret press down against her heart. He'd said that he loved her, and she'd thrown it all away for an unworthy man.

She couldn't lie to herself any longer. She did love James. Even when she kept trying to convince herself that she loved Kyle, her steadfast heart knew otherwise.

But she had hurt him terribly, and she couldn't blame him if he never wanted to see her again.

Abby didn't arrive back at the boardinghouse until nine o'clock at night.

When she stepped down from the cab, she immediately looked up at James's window, hoping to see his light on, praying that he had changed his mind about leaving.

No light shone from the window. The curtains weren't

even drawn. The room looked dark and empty. Uninhabited.

But the parlor lights glowed softly from behind drawn curtains downstairs. She listened for piano music, thinking that he and Josie were enjoying a musical evening. Not a sound.

After paying the cab driver, who carried her luggage up the stairs, Abby unlocked the front door and called out, "Josie? I'm home."

She started when Josie's neighbor appeared in the parlor doorway. "Mrs. Gray, you gave me a fright."

"Sorry," the woman replied. "Josie's not here. Her sister's sick, and she went to Evanston to be with her. She didn't say how long she'd be, but she asked me to look after the house until you got back."

"Where's Mr. Bradshaw?" Abby asked. "The other boarder."

"Josie told me he moved out."

James was gone, as he'd promised. If he really loved her, why hadn't he stayed?

She looked around the foyer. "Where's Ulysses?" He usually came to greet her the minute she walked through the door.

"Come to think of it, I haven't seen your cat, either," Mrs. Gray said, taking her coat off the rack. "Maybe he snuck out when I wasn't looking."

Abby felt the blood drain from her face. The thought of Ulysses, a house cat not used to the dangerous city streets, being lost . . . She pushed the thought from her mind.

"Well," Mrs. Gray said, "now that you're here, I'll be on my way."

Abby thanked her for looking after the house, and the neighbor left.

After the door closed, Abby locked it and checked the downstairs rooms, calling Ulysses' name. No cat trotted out to greet her with his tail held high or a mouse hanging from his jaws. She went upstairs. Surely she would find him in James's room, sitting patiently, waiting for mice.

She turned on the light and felt once again that she was tumbling down Alice's rabbit hole.

James's bed was made. No books and notebooks cluttered the desk's pristine surface. Abby opened his armoire, expecting to find it filled with his clothes. Empty. Not even Lizzie's watercolor still hung on the wall.

With a sinking heart, Abby crossed the hall to her own room. When she turned on the light, she immediately noticed the envelope anchored by the cat figurine on her desk.

She recognized James's handwriting, and tore open the envelope. She sat down at the window seat and began reading.

He said that by the time she returned from Little Falls, he'd be gone, as he promised. Considering his feelings for her, he couldn't bear to stay in the same house with her knowing she belonged to another.

There was more, but blinding tears made it impossible to read. Until Abby got to the end.

As you suspected, Shays hired those men to abduct you. I asked Nick to investigate for me, and he learned their identities. Now that you know, I hope your nightmares will end.

James.

His final gift to her. What it must have cost him to swallow his pride and ask his father for such a favor.

She leaned her head back and let the tears stream down her cheeks. She'd lost everything. Kyle. James. Even her cat.

She still had her veterinary career. She was still valedictorian.

But without someone to share it with, even that no longer mattered.

19

"WHERE IS MISS COOPER?" DR. HOGG DEMANDED.

James stood before his professor's desk after the rest of the class had left. "She's back from visiting her family in Missouri, but I don't know why she hasn't been attending classes."

The day classes resumed after spring break, James had expected to see her sitting in the back row, as usual. But she never showed up. Another day passed. No Abby.

Yesterday, James, frantic with worry that she was ill or hurt, had gone to the boardinghouse looking for her. No one answered the doorbell, and on the day he moved out, he had relinquished his key to Josie, so he couldn't let himself in. When he asked the neighbors for information, they told him that Mrs. Wachowski was staying with her sick sister in Evanston, but that Miss Cooper had returned. They had seen her walking in the neighborhood just that morning.

James waited for several hours, but wherever Abby had gone, she was taking her sweet time getting home. Discouraged, he finally left.

Whatever her reasons for not attending classes, at least

he knew she was home and had come to no harm.

Hogg's boar-bristle eyebrows rose, and he did not look pleased. "As you know, I've scheduled a major test on all new material for the day after tomorrow. This test will count for half your grade. Anyone who fails it will surely fail my course."

Since Abby hadn't been attending classes, she wasn't learning the new material. As James could attest, Dr. Hogg had covered much new ground in his lectures, and most of it difficult.

The professor adjusted his bow tie. "Miss Cooper is my best student, but even so, she's too far behind at this point to pass this test. She will fail my course. And she won't graduate." He shook his head. "That would be such a shame."

"She will be in class tomorrow," James said. "I'll see to it myself." If he had to drag her.

He strode out.

James didn't let the light spring rain deter him as he marched across campus. He had Abby on his mind.

He had been such a fool to let her go. But she'd insisted she loved Lambert and planned to marry him. James had taken her at her word.

He'd paid a high price.

As he'd told her in his letter, he'd found himself another boardinghouse, one without a dark-haired beauty across the hall or a pesky, temperamental cat always trying to sneak into his room. But Abby's sweet ghost haunted and taunted him day and night.

Whenever he looked up at Lizzie's watercolor hanging on the wall over his new desk, his mind's eye conjured up visions of Abby in her father's old shirt, and a pair of dungarees sheathing her mile-high legs. He remembered her kisses, hot and sweet, and the feel of her pliant body pressed against his. Then the yearning would tear at his heart like sharp cat claws.

Life with her, without having her, was sheer hell. Life without her was worse. He wished he had never left Josie's boardinghouse.

What had Nick said? *If you're not going to fight, then you'll settle for what you get.*

Nobility hadn't gotten him anywhere.

He couldn't settle for a life without Abby.

Determination quickened James's step as he turned down another street. He intended to confront her. He intended to make her admit to herself that she really loved him and they belonged together.

If he had to lock her away in Nick's house until she came to her senses, he would.

Abby ran up the boardinghouse's slick front steps and unlocked the door, eager to get out of the pouring rain.

Once inside the foyer, she took off her raincoat and hung it up to dry, leaving puddles on Josie's clean floor. Abby didn't care about the floor. She cared more about James, and finding Ulysses.

With each passing day, that prospect grew dimmer and dimmer. Abby refused to give up hope, though four days had passed since she returned to Chicago from spring break and found both James and her cat gone.

When she wasn't roaming the streets, looking for any sign of Ulysses in alleyways, knocking on doors asking if anyone had seen a black-and-white cat, she sat alone in her room, holding the cat figurine and thinking of James.

He haunted her.

Abby went into the kitchen to make herself a cup of hot tea. She wished she had listened to her innermost

desires and spent spring break with him. She had been
such a fool to deny the overpowering mutual attraction.
But she'd promised herself to Kyle, and she always honored her promises.

And Kyle had proven himself unworthy.

After one week with James, Abby knew she'd be lost.
He'd woo her, charm her, seduce her, challenge her.
They would inevitably become lovers. Once that happened, she would belong to him forever. Now she belonged to no man.

It's not too late, her little voice whispered. *Go to him.
Tell him you love him.*

The tea kettle shrieked. Abby took it off the burner
and strode out of the kitchen. In the foyer, she took her
raincoat off the rack and put it on.

She had to find James.

The light mist had changed to a heavy downpour by the
time James turned down Abby's street. The rain pelted
his face and ran down his neck in cold rivulets, his
turned-up coat collar affording him scant protection
against the persistent gray wall of water. But he ignored
the discomfort of feeling half drowned.

Abby was worth any discomfort.

At four o'clock in the afternoon, cabs, carriages, and
freight wagons rattled up and down the street, their
wheels spinning through puddles as their drivers tried to
make one last delivery before the end of the day. James
looked up and down the street carefully before he
crossed, and stepped back lest he be splashed.

As he approached the boardinghouse, his spirits plum-
meted. The house looked dark and shuttered, with no
light shining in the parlor window. This time, he would
wait for Abby if he had to stand in the rain all night.

Perhaps he could wait in Kachinsky's. At least he'd be warm and dry.

He was just about to cross the street when he saw a black-and-white cat come streaking out of the butcher shop's side alley.

Ulysses? What was he doing outside on a rainy afternoon? Abby never let him out of the house. The streets were far too dangerous for her precious pet.

The cat didn't stop at the curb.

James watched in mounting horror as Ulysses gambled all nine of his lives by making a run for it across the street, unmindful of the carriages and wagons going back and forth, water spraying up from their wheels.

He darted beneath one carriage and barely got his tail brushed by its spinning wheels. He didn't move fast enough to avoid a second carriage coming in the opposite direction.

A wheel caught him.

Ulysses yowled, and rolled.

The cat hadn't come to a stop before James ran into the rain-slick street, unmindful of the traffic himself. A driver sawed on the reins to halt his horse just in time, and shouted curses and threats, but James ignored him.

He picked up Ulysses' bleeding, limp body and carried him to the safety of the sidewalk.

One cursory look told James that both the cat's femur and tibia of its bloody right hind leg had been crushed by the carriage's wheel.

But Ulysses was still alive. In shock, but alive.

"Hang on, General," James said, cradling him in his arms. "We're going to get you some help."

As James strode toward the boardinghouse, the front door opened and Abby emerged.

• • •

Abby was turning to lock the front door when she heard an urgent, familiar voice call her name.

She turned, locking the front door forgotten. Her pulse raced. She smiled. *James.*

He wore no hat, so the pouring rain plastered his dark hair to his head in a sleek helmet, and formed tears on the tips of his thick eyelashes. He looked cold, wet, and miserable, but to Abby, he was the most wonderful sight in the world.

Then she saw what he held.

A sodden, limp rag of black-and-white fur splattered with blood.

Ulysses.

An anguished scream of denial welled up inside her, but when she opened her mouth, only a whimper escaped her compressed lips.

"He tried to run across the street," James said over the hiss of the rain, "but a carriage hit him. We've got to get him inside before he bleeds to death."

Abby opened the front door, strode through the foyer, and started up the stairs. "Bring him into the kitchen. I'll get a blanket."

When she came back down with a blanket for her cat and a towel for James, she found he'd laid the cat on one of Josie's tea towels and was tying a piece of twine as a tourniquet high on its leg to stop the bleeding.

James glanced over at her, unmindful of the water dripping off his chin. "The carriage wheel crushed his leg."

Abby looked down at her beloved pet, his green eyes shocked slits, his breathing quick and shallow, and she petted his wet head. She crooned endearments to soothe him while she examined the shattered leg as carefully and gently as she could.

Helpless tears filled her eyes. She took a deep shuddering breath. "The leg can't be saved."

"You'll have to amputate," James said. He shrugged out of his wet coat and draped it over one of the chairs. Then he quickly dried his face and hair with the towel. "He probably won't be fast enough to catch any more mice, but at least he'll be alive."

Hope flooded through Abby as she looked down at her cat. Ulysses had been her friend and constant companion ever since she'd come to Chicago to go to veterinary school. He'd slept by her side every night, and he awakened her every morning. When she became despondent, his comical smudged face cheered her up. He hunted mice and presented them to her as tribute. He asked for so little in return.

She looked at James. "I've never done an amputation on a live animal."

"Neither have I." He grasped her shoulders and stared deeply into her eyes as if seeking to pull out the courage he knew to be there. "You're better at performing surgery than I am. I'd never forgive myself if the General died because I made a mistake."

"I don't know if I can. He's my pet."

He gave her a little shake. "You can do it. I know you can."

"Would we have time to get him over to the college's surgery?"

"Classes are over for the day, and it's locked up."

Abby took another deep breath and steeled herself. "Then we'll have to do it here. I'll get my bag. You boil some water."

When she came back downstairs, she set her bag on the counter and prepared to anesthetize Ulysses. In school, cats that were to be anesthetized were placed in a box with a glass in its lid. Chloroform was introduced gradually on pieces of cotton wool dropped into the box. The excitement stage, consisting of the cat's meowing and struggling before accepting the inevitable and falling unconscious, could be observed through the box's glass top. Unfortunately, Abby had no glass-topped box. She would have to make do with an ordinary cardboard box that had once held her sewing supplies.

She lined the box with another tea towel. James gently picked up the cat and set him inside.

"I wish we had some ether to mix with the chloroform," she said to James as she poured several drops on a piece of cotton wool. The mixture was usually safer than pure chloroform for cats.

"No time," he replied. "We'll have to do the best we can with what we've got, and hope for the best."

James busied himself preparing and setting out the instruments and sutures Abby would need.

She put the cloth in the box with Ulysses, and put the cover back on.

She waited. Fresh tears welled in her eyes when she heard the cat's feeble struggle against the inevitable loss of consciousness. Then the chloroform did its work.

Abby removed the cover, taking care not to breathe the fumes herself, and James placed the unconscious cat on the blanket spread out on the kitchen table.

"You look pale. Will you be able to go through with this?"

She went to the sink to wash her hands. "I have to."

"Don't think about Ulysses as your pet," James said. "Just concentrate on the procedure."

When she returned to the table, she examined Ulysses' hip to see if it had been fractured. She was relieved to find that it hadn't, so she proceeded.

She decided to amputate high, near Ulysses' hip, a point well above and clear of the most damage.

James swabbed the area with antiseptic. "Are you going to use the elliptical flap or the circular flap method?"

"Elliptical," she replied.

"Dr. Emerson claims it's better," James said.

Taking the scalpel, Abby incised the skin and other soft tissues, cutting the latter to form a smaller flap than that formed by the skin. She moved the soft tissues away from the bone and back.

She asked James for the saw.

"I'm sorry, old friend," she murmured, glancing at her unconscious pet.

James touched her shoulder with a comforting hand. "Concentrate on the procedure."

Abby steeled herself against the rasp of the saw severing bone, and proceeded to amputate Ulysses' leg.

When it was over, she stood back and took a deep, shuddering breath. "I'm going to release the tourniquet. Will you tie off the bleeders?"

"That I can do."

Once that was completed, Abby drew the flaps over the stump and secured them with interrupted sutures. James applied the antiseptic dressing.

Since Ulysses usually slept where he liked, he had no basket to serve as a bed, so Abby folded the blanket, set it down by the kitchen stove, and tenderly laid her unconscious cat there.

She looked over at James, who was cleaning up. God, she had missed him! She wanted to cross the room and fling herself in his arms, but she wasn't sure how he'd react after the way she'd rejected and hurt him.

When Abby saw him shudder, she realized that the shoulders of his shirt were soaked through, as were the legs of his trousers where rain had blown under his coat. He'd assisted her with surgery while wearing wet clothes.

"You're shivering," she said.

"It's cold in here," he said between gritted teeth. "Don't you have any heat in this house?"

"It's spring. Josie turned it off for the season."

James shuddered again.

"You'd better get out of those wet clothes," Abby said.

He raised his brows. "And what am I going to wear while they're drying? I moved out, remember, and took my clothes with me."

"You could wear my kimono." A smile tugged at her mouth at the thought of tall, broad James in her robe.

She also remembered the night she and James had come down to the kitchen for hot milk, and she'd burned herself. The kimono sleeve had fallen back, so he could kiss her wrist. Her smile died.

James must have remembered, too, for his night-dark eyes sparkled, and he reached for her hand. This time, it was her left hand.

"Where's Kyle's ring?" he said softly.

"Another woman's wearing it."

First came shocked surprise. Then hope as bright as fire lit his features. "Does that mean you're not marrying him?"

"That's what it means."

He drew her hand to his lips and kissed her bare fourth finger. "So you're free."

"Free?" A hysterical bubble of laughter escaped her lips. "I haven't been free since the day I met you."

He grew very still and studied her, his expression inscrutable. He wouldn't let go of her hand. "About time you realized it."

Then he pulled her into his arms and began devouring her like a starving man. He kissed her forehead, her eyelids, and finally her mouth. There was no gentleness, no tentativeness this time. His assault on her senses became an exultant claiming.

She felt his lips part for a sensual, openmouthed kiss, and she responded in kind, gasping at the unfamiliar sensation of his tongue invading her mouth. The joining sent her reeling, as if the kitchen floor had suddenly fallen away, with only his arms to keep her from the abyss.

When they parted, breathless and panting, he stroked her cheeks with his thumbs, tracing her high cheekbones as if committing them to memory.

"I meant it when I said I love you," he said.

"I've been such an idiot." Abby slid her arms around his waist and hugged him. "All the time I thought I loved Kyle, I really loved you, but I couldn't dare admit it, especially to myself."

He shivered again, though Abby suspected it had nothing to do with the damp, rainy day, the cool kitchen, and his wet clothes.

She released him. "You'd better change before you catch pneumonia." Her voice trembled. "I don't want to lose you just when I've found you."

"I'm still not wearing your kimono."

"Then wrap yourself in a blanket and come back downstairs. I'll make some tea."

He headed for the door, then turned. "I want something hotter than tea tonight."

She smiled, finally sure of herself and what she wanted. "You'll get it."

His deep, lascivious chuckle filled the kitchen, and she blushed.

Abby fought back unshed tears as she looked out into the wet street where Ulysses had almost died. She closed the curtains to find James standing in the parlor doorway, barefoot, with a tan blanket wrapped around him like a long shawl that came down almost to his ankles.

"I draped my clothes over the kitchen chairs to dry," he said. "Ulysses is still unconscious, but his heartbeat's strong and he's alive."

"Thank you for saving him. If you hadn't come along when you did, he would've bled to death in the gutter."

James padded across the room, his bare feet soundless on the carpet. "He's going to be fine. You know yourself that cats and dogs adapt quite well to three legs."

"I know." She paused. "Why did you come here today? After you moved out, I thought I'd never see you again—except in class."

He gave her an exasperated look. "In case you haven't noticed, you haven't been to class in the last four days. Piggy Hogg has a big test on all new material planned for the day after tomorrow, and he's afraid you'll fail."

Abby blanched. "I had too much on my mind to attend class."

He reached out and traced the line of her jaw with his fingertips. "I was half crazy with worry. And I came here intending to fight for you."

She felt absurdly pleased. "Fight for me?"

"To woo you and win you. Nick's been giving me pointers, but even he draws the line at locking you away in a tower and ravishing you until you agree to marry me."

"You don't need to lock me away to get me to agree to marry you." And as for the ravishment part . . .

James grinned. "If that's a proposal, I accept."

Abby rolled her eyes and groaned. "You're incorrigible. Drink your tea."

Once they were seated on the sofa, Abby poured tea into the new cups James had given Josie, and handed him one, trying to keep her eyes off his naked torso.

"Now," he said, "tell me what happened in Little Falls."

Abby told him about Kyle and Mary Dobbs.

"He only wanted me as a means of getting the saloon," she said. "But Mary's family is providing that now, so she saved me from making the biggest mistake of my life."

James's eyes grew cold. "Even if he hadn't betrayed you, I would've found a way to keep you from marrying him."

"Don't be angry with me for saying this, but you're more like your father than you want to admit, James Bradshaw."

He leaned over and kissed her gently. "I'm discovering that I can be just as ruthless when I want something badly enough."

Abby snuggled closer and boldly slipped her hand beneath the edge of his blanket, running her fingers across the smooth, silky hairs of his bare chest in a delicate caress. "So can I."

His eyes darkened impossibly, and he regarded her from beneath partially lowered lids. "And to think I once called you the Ice Maiden."

Abby felt as though he'd slapped her. She jerked her hand away and would have stood, but James was too quick for her.

He grasped her wrist to keep her from fleeing. "What's wrong? What did I do?"

"Kyle called me an icicle," she said, her voice trembling. "He said I couldn't get a man hot if I was set on fire."

James tugged on her wrist, causing her to fall across his lap. "Lambert's an ass. And so am I, for even thinking that. I only called you that because you were always so cool and remote in class. But as I got to know you, I learned you weren't an Ice Maiden at all." He brushed her mouth with his own. "Quite the contrary."

Abby stared over his shoulder and debated telling him about her encounter with Kyle in the barn. She decided that if they were to have an honest and open relationship, she had to confess her deepest secret.

"When I was home last summer," she began, unable to look him in the eye, "Kyle and I went out to my grandmother's barn. He . . . took liberties, and I let him."

"So you did make love to him." Cold, hard jealousy edged his voice. "I'd always wondered."

Abby's eyes widened in indignation and she tried to pull away. "I did *not*! How could you even think that I—!"

He grinned, held her fast around the waist despite her squirming, and nipped her chin. "You *almost* made love to him."

"Yes," she admitted, blushing. "And it didn't feel as wonderful as I thought it would, as my mama told me it would be."

"Abby, you silly puss, look at me."

She sighed and did as he bade her.

"It didn't feel as wonderful as you thought because you were sharing intimacies with the wrong man."

She blinked. "Is that the reason?"

"I'll prove it to you," he whispered, "if you'll let me."

She smiled slowly, and pushed the blanket off his shoulders, admiring the pale skin and sleek muscle, silk over steel. "At Christmas, my little Lizard said she wanted to paint you in the nude."

He grinned. "She did?"

"Mm-hmm. I was so jealous I could feel myself turning green. She went on and on about your black, windswept hair, your handsome, brooding face, your broad, muscular shoulders, your sensuous mouth. I told her that when you took off your clothes for a woman, it wasn't to have your portrait painted."

He nibbled on her earlobe. "You were right. If you come upstairs with me, I'll show you exactly what I do when I take off my clothes for a woman."

20

"UNLESS YOU WANT TO WAIT UNTIL WE'RE MARried," he added.

Comfortably ensconced on his lap, Abby leaned her elbows against his bare shoulders so she could run her fingers through his thick, damp hair. Then she pulled his head back so she could plunder his mouth with her own.

When she released him, she said, "When would we get married?"

"In June, after graduation."

She looked up at the ceilings, calculating the arithmetic in her head. "That's a little more than another month."

"Five weeks." His kissed the hollow of her throat. "An eternity."

"I can't wait that long."

A devilish twinkle lit his eyes. "You were willing to wait that long for Kyle."

"I wasn't in a hurry because, deep down inside, I knew he wasn't the right man for me." She traced what Grandmama Maddy would call his "sweet kissing mouth" with her little finger. "He never liked Ulysses, you see, and the feeling was mutual."

"You should always listen to your cat," he said. "He's an excellent judge of character."

She smiled. "I know. You're lucky he likes you. Otherwise . . ." She let her voice trail off.

"I am lucky."

She leaned forward, and whispered, "Let's go upstairs," in his ear.

Then she slid off his lap and extended her hand. He rose, his blanket still draped around him like a long shawl. Without warning, he opened the blanket and wrapped it around both of them, enfolding her in his bare arms and the warm, dark cocoon.

She got a quick, tantalizing flash of his naked body, then he was holding her, surrounding her, and she saw no more. Her arms slipped around his narrow waist, and she rested her blushing cheek against his shoulder, breathing in his own unique warm, spicy masculine scent.

"You'll have to forgive me if I seem awkward and don't know what to do," she murmured, all too aware of his hips and groin pressing against her skirt. "I've watched animals mating, but I never—"

"Take your time. Touch me any way you like. I won't be shocked."

"But I will be."

She ran her hands up and down his back, all warm, hard muscle at the shoulders, with a vulnerable dip at the lower back. Emboldened by his sigh, she stroked lower, running her hands down his sleek, firm backside.

He groaned. "You learn fast."

"I like touching you," she said shyly. "You're so smooth and hard."

He kissed the top of her head.

Being wrapped in the blanket with him eased her

nervousness, for she could learn the feel of him to her heart's content without feeling exposed herself.

Finally, when he let go of the blanket so he could cup her face in his hands and kiss her with aching tenderness, she was prepared for his nakedness.

When they parted, she first kept her gaze on his handsome face, but then her curiosity got the better of her. Her gaze slid lower to his flat belly. And lower still.

She gulped, turned red, and looked away. Dear God, he was large. For a man, she supposed. Her standards of comparison having been limited to stallions and bulls.

She looked at the parlor windows. "I'm glad I drew the curtains."

"Let's go upstairs," he said. "We'll have more privacy there."

Her bedroom was bathed in the light of late afternoon, diminished even more by gray, low-hanging clouds and torrents of rain drumming against the roof and windows. In the weak light, the bedroom was as warm and cozy as the blanket cocoon.

She stood there, watching him, overcome with shyness again and wondering what came next. Soon she and this man would share their bodies intimately, and reveal their innermost souls to each other.

"Having second thoughts?" he said gently.

She managed a tremulous smile. "Does it show?"

"If you'd rather wait, I—"

"I wouldn't."

He stared at her with an intensity that sent her heart racing and tripping, and made her weak in the knees. She felt herself drown in the night sky of those eyes.

He started unbuttoning her shirtwaist. "I thought when I first undressed you I'd be taking off your father's shirt and your dungarees."

"You'd never seen a woman in trousers before?"

He unbuttoned the last button and shook his head. "You don't know what those dungarees did to me, Abigail Cooper."

"Aroused you?" was her bold reply. As she was arousing him so obviously now.

"Violently." He unbuttoned her skirt next, pushing it off her hips and down to the floor, where it puddled at her ankles. "I couldn't stop thinking of your long, beautiful legs."

Kyle had never complimented her legs. She blushed with pleasure that James had noticed, and approved.

He undressed her faster now, with impatience, but still with finesse. Down came her underskirt. When he drew her lacy camisole over her head, baring her breasts, she blushed and had to fight the urge to cross her arms over herself in modesty.

She loved this man. She wanted to hide nothing from him. She wanted him to know everything about her.

"You are so beautiful," he whispered, his hot gaze searing her breasts. He touched them with a gentleness that made her gasp.

Then he lowered his head and nuzzled the taut crest with his lips, teasing it until she groaned. When he finally suckled the straining nipple, she cried out as her blood turned to fire in her veins.

His fingers dove into her hair, seeking and pulling out hairpins until the tresses flowed down her shoulders like dark, soft silk. Then his skillful hands made even shorter work of her drawers and stockings.

When she finally stood completely naked before him, surprisingly, her shyness left her. The way he was looking at her made her feel oddly powerful, like some ancient queen or goddess revered by her subjects.

He kissed her until she thought she would faint from the pleasure.

He squeezed her breast. "Now that we've set you on fire, I'm going to prove to you that you can make a man burn."

He took her hand and led her over to the bed. He pulled back the covers and slid in, drawing her against him so she faced the opposite direction.

"Close your eyes," he whispered.

His tongue darted into her ear. She shuddered and gasped at the delicious sensation. He slipped his hands beneath her arms so her could caress her breasts as he trailed erotic kisses down her neck and sensitive back, all the while whispering praises to her beauty.

When his lips and tongue and fingers and love words had aroused her to the point of madness, she turned to face him. He smiled and kissed her again, deeply, while his teasing, exploring fingers moved between her thighs.

One touch sent her over the edge. She shuddered and convulsed as she knew ecstasy in her lover's arms.

He chuckled as she sighed, closed her eyes, and snuggled against him, spent. But he didn't let her rest for long.

"My turn," he whispered, gently nipping her chin. "I want you to tell me what you're going to do to me. Then do it."

Her cheeks burned at the very suggestion, but she did as he bade her. To her astonishment, she found verbalizing and carrying out what she had imagined not only diminished her inhibitions, but violently aroused both her and James.

Mindless with longing when she gave herself to him, she barely felt the initial pain of his physical possession.

All she knew was the rapture of their joining as they rocked and rocked and rocked.

She knew ecstasy first, crying out his name as she shuddered over and over and over. Before she drifted down, he called to her, and knew rapture as well.

Much later, when the dwindling afternoon slipped into evening, and only the streetlight below illuminated the room, Abby propped herself up on one elbow and looked down at her drowsy, satisfied lover.

"Lizzie told me that an old Chinese woman she knows in San Francisco told her that when two people love each other, they give each other gifts. The gift can be an occurrence that makes them realize they love each other, or the gifts come later in life, bearing messages or lessons." She ran her fingertips along his chest. "Kyle's never given me such gifts. You have."

James frowned. "What gifts have I given you, except for the figurine at Christmas?"

"You learned that Shays was behind my abduction after all, even though you hate to ask your father for favors."

"I didn't think of it as a gift. I just thought if you knew, your nightmares would stop."

She smiled. "I know they will. Now."

He reached up to brush a lock of hair away from her damp, flushed cheek. "You could report him to the police. Nick has the evidence."

"I could, but we'll be graduating soon, and I'll never see him again. I want to put it behind me."

"I can understand that."

"And you've proven to me that I'm not an icicle or an ice maiden after all."

"My pleasure, ma'am," he said with a teasing grin,

his gaze heating up again as it roved leisurely over her body. "Definitely my pleasure."

A plaintive meow from the doorway caused them both to sit up and look in the doorway.

A scraggly, bewildered, drowsy Ulysses stood there.

"Oh, my poor darling," Abby crooned, getting out of bed and hurrying over to her cat. "You shouldn't have climbed those stairs so soon after surgery."

Ulysses stared up at Abby and meowed loudly as if to demand what had happened to him.

She lifted him gently into her arms, savoring his warmth. "I'm sorry," she whispered, taking care not to touch his bandaged stump, "but I had no choice. You would've died." Hot tears stung her eyes. "Will you forgive me?"

Ulysses rubbed his face against her cheek and purred loudly. Relieved, Abby took him over to the bed, and they rejoined James.

She looked at the man she loved. "And you saved my cat." Abby scratched Ulysses under the chin. "What gifts have I given you, except aggravation?"

James petted Ulysses' head. "You gave me the serenity of Little Falls. And you convinced me that if I ever want to be at peace with myself, I have to separate my father from his violent world, and what he does."

"Nick may have a dark side, and he may have done terrible, unpardonable things, but he is your father, and he does love you."

He kissed her bare shoulder. "And you've given me the biggest gift of all by agreeing to become my wife."

James moved back to the boardinghouse and into his old room that night. But he didn't have sleeping on his mind. Or lovemaking.

"Enough of this," he said sternly, grasping Abby's wrists to keep her from entwining her arms around his neck and kissing him again. "You have to study."

She pouted. "I'd much rather—" When she told him, *he* blushed.

He shook his head. "This is what happens when you educate women."

Abby stuck her tongue out at him, and kissed him anyway.

James rolled his eyes. "If I give you something, will you promise to study?"

"I promise."

He reached into his coat pocket and pulled out the blue velvet box Nick had given him. He opened it and showed the ring to Abby.

Her eyes widened. "Oh, James, it's beautiful!"

"It was my mother's favorite ring," he said, taking it out of the box. "Nick gave it to me to give to the woman I planned to marry." He took Abby's hand and slipped the sapphire on her finger, delighted to replace Lambert's ring. "Nick knew the day he met you that you were the woman for me."

Abby held out her hand, admiring the sparkling large blue stone with its surround of diamonds. "Smart man." She kissed his cheek, her blue eyes as bright as her sapphire. "Thank you. I'd be honored to wear your mother's ring."

He pulled his books and notes out of his bag and set them on the kitchen table. "Piggy's test is the day after tomorrow, and you have a lot of catching up to do."

They sat down at the kitchen table and studied until Abby couldn't keep her eyes open. James stuffed the material into her head like the filling in one of Josie's stuffed cabbages. When they finally went to bed exhausted, they retired to their respective bedrooms.

The following day, Abby resumed her classes, explaining to her professors that she'd been ill. Luckily they accepted her excuse.

Finally came the day of Dr. Hogg's infectious-diseases exam.

When the interminable test was over and the professor collected their papers, James whispered to Abby, "How did you do?"

She shrugged somberly. "I don't know. Those questions were tough. Your helping me study certainly made a big difference."

He smiled. "What are fiancés for?"

Both Abby and James spent the rest of the day and evening on pins and needles. They got little sleep, knowing that if Abby failed this test, she'd fail Dr. Hogg's class. And if she failed Dr. Hogg's class, she wouldn't graduate.

When they arrived at class the following morning, they walked to the head of the classroom and sat in the front row. Abby decided that if she went down in flames today, she'd go down with her head held high and her back to the men who had disapproved and tormented her.

She mentally dared any of them to shoot a spitball into her hair. Not with her fiancé seated beside her.

Dr. Hogg came in with the tests under his arm and greeted everyone cheerfully.

Abby held her breath and prayed.

Dr. Hogg stopped in front of her desk and stared down at her. He handed her the test.

"Congratulations, Miss Cooper."

She looked at James and smiled. Now she had everything she'd ever wanted.

EPILOGUE

Maddy sat between Cat and Jace, looking at all the people in the audience, eager for Abby's outdoor graduation ceremony in the college's quadrangle to begin.

She was glad she wore one of her fancy New York outfits with a wide-brimmed tea-party hat to keep the warm June sun off her face. So many in the audience were dressed in their finery. Maddy would have hated to look like a Missouri bumpkin among all these sophisticated city folk. She had her pride.

She glanced to her left. Even Jace looked natty today, sitting and talking to Josie, who sat at his left and kept weeping into her handkerchief. Maddy had seen several silver-haired women giving him surreptitious glances from beneath their wide-brimmed hats. That's all they needed, to turn the old rogue loose among the ladies of Chicago. He'd never go home.

Cat, who'd traded her dungarees and shirt for a dress today, grasped Maddy's hand and squeezed. "Today's the day, Mama." Her eyes sparkled with tears of happiness. "Today our Abby becomes a real veterinarian."

Maddy sighed and brushed away a tear or two of her own. "I wish your father had lived long enough to see this day. He'd be so proud of her."

"He is. I just know he's up in heaven looking down on us today."

"With Zeke by his side." Waiting for Maddy to join them.

Soon, she thought.

"The Reverend Dawlish always said that animals don't go to heaven," Cat said.

"I'm sure he's getting the surprise of his life," Maddy said with a disrespectful snort, for the good reverend had gone to his eternal reward just last month.

Maddy sighed. "Times sure have changed, haven't they, Catherine? This country had only one veterinary school when your father wanted to doctor animals, and when they finally did get some, they wouldn't admit women. Now here's your daughter, the first woman to graduate from the Chicago Veterinary College."

Cat glanced at Michael sitting to her right, studying his program. "As happy as I am that Abby's graduating, I'm just as happy that she's found such a good man as James."

Maddy thought of her beloved Paul. "Life sure is sweeter when you have someone to share it with."

Jace stirred by Maddy's side. "Here they come."

The band started playing, and the graduates marched onto the dais and took their places.

Abby, from her special valedictorian's seat in the front row next to James, could clearly see her family and Josie sitting in the audience. Grandpapa Jace, Grandmama Maddy, and Abby's parents. Regina had wanted to come, but had a one-month-old baby boy at home to keep her busy. Lizzie was still in San Francisco, though she'd be home in time for Abby and James's wedding.

Abby smiled at them and gave a little wave. They all waved back.

She tried to keep her mind on the ceremony, but couldn't stop thinking of another ceremony that would take place in two weeks in Little Falls—her marriage ceremony.

Dr. Abigail Cooper Bradshaw. Mrs. James Bradshaw.

Both titles fit her so well, she thought, since she was both women. And more.

Before she knew it, the graduation ceremony was over.

"Congratulations, Dr. Cooper," James said with a wide grin, giving her a quick kiss.

She thought of Dr. Hogg's exam. "I couldn't have done it without you, Dr. Bradshaw."

"Your family's waiting. Let's get out of here and celebrate."

Before she started down the dais steps, Abby turned and caught Rockwell Shays's eye. She couldn't resist. She raised her fist in a gesture of triumph, her diploma held tightly in her hand.

Shays just scowled at her once before turning away.

As Abby and James started down the dais steps, she saw Nick standing in the back behind the seated guests. Abby had invited him, but she wasn't sure that he'd come. He turned and started walking away.

Abby exchanged looks with James.

She watched as the man she loved with all her heart fought his way through the throng of well-wishers. He caught up with his father on the edge of the quadrangle.

Abby watched the two men stand and talk together for all the world to see.

Then both headed back to join her.

TIME PASSAGES

___CRYSTAL MEMORIES   Ginny Aiken   0-515-12159-2

___A DANCE THROUGH TIME   Lynn Kurland

                                           0-515-11927-X

___ECHOES OF TOMORROW   Jenny Lykins   0-515-12079-0

___LOST YESTERDAY   Jenny Lykins   0-515-12013-8

___MY LADY IN TIME   Angie Ray   0-515-12227-0

___NICK OF TIME   Casey Claybourne   0-515-12189-4

___REMEMBER LOVE   Susan Plunkett   0-515-11980-6

___SILVER TOMORROWS   Susan Plunkett   0-515-12047-2

___THIS TIME TOGETHER   Susan Leslie Liepitz

                                           0-515-11981-4

___WAITING FOR YESTERDAY   Jenny Lykins

                                           0-515-12129-0

___HEAVEN'S TIME   Susan Plunkett   0-515-12287-4